DATE DUE			

What's

Inside

You

It

Shines

Out

of

You

What's
Inside
You

Horizon Press ▷ New York

It

Shines

Out

of

You

by Marc Kaminsky

For my grandparents
Alter and Esther Schwartzman
Yashiah and Bluma Kaminsky

Library of Congress Cataloging in Publication Data

Kaminsky, Marc, 1943-
  What's inside of you it shines out of you.

  Includes bibliographical references.
  1. Poetry — Study and teaching.   2. Poetry —
Authorship.   3. Poetry — Therapeutic use.   4. Aged —
Recreation.   I. Title.
PN1101.K25   811'.5'409   74-8779
ISBN 0-8180-1568-3

Acknowledgments

I am deeply indebted to the friends and colleagues who read the manuscript and offered valuable comments and suggestions: Allan Appel, Dr. John Beletsis, Riva Danzig, Paul Gorrin, Dr. Jack Leedy, Phillip Lopate, Peretz Kaminsky, Mel Konner, David Soyer, Carol Talesnick, Laura Vajda.

I am also deeply appreciative of the encouragement which I received from the Jewish Association for Services for the Aged, through a grant funded by the Human Resources Administration and the Federation of Jewish Philanthropies. I am particularly grateful to Rabbi Jerome Fishman, Sam Hock, Adele Trobe and Bernard Warach. Their co-operation was vital to the Poetry Program.

Steve Schrader and Glenda Adams of the Teachers & Writers Collaborative gave generously of their time and energies to the program, and also arranged for a grant, through the New York State Council on the Arts, under which Part Two of this book was written.

I would also like to thank Norm Danzig, who took the cover photographs, and Peretz Kaminsky, who designed the book jacket.

Ben Raeburn's "warm eye" and his "cold eye," his rare combination of sympathy and judgment, have been invaluable to me in recasting the work into its final form.

Contents

The Young Israel Group

The Poems

Part One

Part Two

The Tuesday Group

The Young Israel Group

Part Three

Part One

Preparing the Ground

1

Making Light of It

In the summer of 1972, I took a job as a group-worker with JASA.*
In order to get a better idea of what I would be doing, I was asked
to visit one of JASA's senior citizens' clubs. So quite early one morning, I found myself standing in the near-empty ballroom of an
Upper West Side synagogue. At one end, there was an ark: a blur
of brown wood, rich velvets and gold lions that seemed to be oddly
afloat in this vast expanse of bright pinewood. At the other end,
there were three long rows of tables that reminded me of khaki
regimentation and mess halls. Here and there, yards apart, a few
old women were sitting. Each one sat alone. There was nothing
between the floating ark and the deserted mess hall but the dance
floor on which I was standing, in distress. Was this a senior citizens'
club? Were these old women the people I would be working with?
Was this the kind of place I would be working in? Things didn't
look so good.

The setting, and my presence there, seemed bizarre. I had
known this feeling before, many times, in many places. The words
that came to me were: at the edge of the world.

An old red-faced woman had come in before all the others.
She sat in a corner, next to a square column. Her hands were folded
in her lap. She seemed like one who expects nothing to happen—

* Jewish Association for Services for the Aged (see page 237).

13

ever again. She seemed content to sit there and wait. She seemed like one who can no longer feel impatience. She seemed to be waiting without waiting. I no longer remember who the others were, then, and how many there were of them. There might have been five, and there might have been fifteen. I felt alone with that red-faced woman in the enormous room.

Since there seemed nothing else to do, I went over to talk to her. I went reluctantly. I sensed: she does not wish to be imposed upon. I sat down next to her. She neither welcomed my greeting nor rebuffed it. She seemed neutral, with respect to the living. She was neither for nor against them. She was beyond them, beyond their toils, beyond me. I felt anything I said would be out of place. I said, "How do you like it here?" "It's nice," she said, in a flat voice. It was neither a voice of despair nor contentment. She was neither at peace nor embattled. She was just an old woman in America, and she used an old American word for saying nothing: nice. It was a nice place, she was having a nice time with nice people. She was speaking without speaking. "And what do you do here?" I asked. "We play bingo." She sat, neither looking at me nor looking away. She was not dead and she was not alive. I left her and returned to the no-man's land, between the ark and the tables.

Other women started coming in. No men. I felt I had entered a world invented by a poet. "Abandon all hope ye who enter here." The women came in, gave their greetings, names and quarters to an expressionless woman who sat at the door, and they each sat down—alone. A hefty woman with a fancy hair-do began moving busily along the rows of tables, carrying a tray full of white plastic: forks and spoons. No knives. And then suddenly it was an hour later and the whole room seemed to be crowded and waiting. For what?

The answer burst through the swinging doors—from the kitchen. He was a middle-aged man who greeted everyone with voluminous cheeriness and carried on private conversation in a subdued roar. What was he so happy about? Well, he was cooking a tremendous soup! The old people were waiting to be fed.

The moment he saw me, he started to explain. The man was an explainer. He was the old hand, the senior staff member, and he immediately explained that I had better have a few extra boxes of Saltine crackers on hand, and a few extra cans of soup, so I would have something to open up, in case I ran out—of food. That was the important thing to prepare myself against. Think of the misery I would cause, if I ran out! I would learn to think in terms of a hundred. I would learn to order everything in bulk. There was so much to learn. He would explain it to me.

He explained that I must stock up on tuna fish but that I must never order tuna fish packed in oil. And he explained the reason why. He explained that out of every pound of cottage cheese I must feed four persons. He reminded me to get the Saltine crackers. He explained the symbols on the labels of jars.

He took me inside the kitchen, showed me how the coffee urns worked, showed me his supply cabinet, and introduced me to the secrets of a well-run closet. He showed me his opaque projector, his treasury box, and his big bags of rice. Then he took me over to his twelve-burner stove and showed me the largest pots I had ever come into contact with. In these pots, he was cooking the vegetable soup! He explained the soup: "You take a basic vegetable soup— always be sure to use Heinz—and you get to work on it, you have to know how to add things, this gives it a whole other flavor. In *this* soup I added four quarts of milk and instant potatoes, which gives it a thicker consistency, and look over there—I added all those cans of vegetables, which also adds to the consistency, plus it gives the soup more protein value. You have to be concerned about the protein value they're getting. And you can be creative, too! Instead of just giving them noodles and soup and cheese, you can combine them—and make a casserole!"

By the time he finished explaining, I felt thoroughly anxious. He no doubt noticed my unsatisfactory response. He promised to take me to the super-market to show me how to shop properly.

Better do something fast: help! I said: "What can I do to help?" There were already too many cooks in the kitchen. It was time to disappear. I wandered back into the enormous room, full of worries about the fine points of feeding an army on a low budget.

One of the women became curious about this unfamiliar young man who seemed as if he had taken a wrong turn in some foreign country and was walking about trying to summon enough Greek to his tongue to ask for directions to the nearest airport. She greeted me warmly, told me her name was Hilda, and asked me what I was doing here. I told her that I had just been hired for a new JASA program, that I would be organizing senior citizens' clubs in Brooklyn, and that I'd be interested in hearing any suggestions she might have to give me. "Well," she began, "you'll have to have cards and bingo, but I'd like something interesting. Senior citizens need something to occupy their minds with. A lot of the women here—they like something that's going to keep their minds active. I myself don't play bingo or cards. A good discussion, a class, that's something I enjoy. Sometimes when the bingo game starts I play Scrabble with another woman. But there's only the two of us. She's a fine woman, a teacher, sometimes she gives us a Hebrew class. I'm very interested to learn."

Suddenly my older colleague was at my side. He explained that there were many "small interest groups" and "mass programs" in the senior citizens' club. There was a newspaper, which the old people put out. There was entertainment, provided by student volunteers. There were lectures, some of which he gave himself. There was singing and dancing, there was arts and crafts, there were picnics, discussions, and a number of games. There were outings, there were films, there were service committees and holiday parties and classes, some of which he taught himself.

He asked me how I would like to take a small group into *that* classroom—he pointed clear across the ballroom, to a closed door—and do something with them. Well, that seemed like a good idea. Did I have any ideas about what I could do? In fact, I did: I would do a poetry workshop.

What struck me, as he walked away, was Hilda's expression. She seemed radiant. She clapped her hands together and let out a small laugh. "I'll let you in on a little secret," she said. "The women here . . . We all have a lot to thank him for."

Six women joined me in the classroom. Hilda was one of them. I remember that her friend, the teacher, was among them. There was also an extremely old and elegant woman named Mary; a tall Austrian woman, a great lady with a long black dress and a string of pearls; an anxious American-born woman, who kept asking me to explain things to her; and a woman whose name and face I forget.

Together with them in a room that neither dwarfed nor pumped up human proportions, I relaxed, I felt back in the world, among people who were familiar to me, engaged in an activity which is so much a part of what I am. I felt a burst of energy, and enjoyed the thought of what was about to take place: the creation of a poem by a group of old people.

I said, "Today we're going to make up a poem together."

They were startled—and interested. They also didn't believe it.

How, they wanted to know, were we going to accomplish this miracle?

If my older colleague had recipes for vegetable soup, I had recipes for poems. Many recipes: they had come, initially, from Kenneth Koch's great cookbook on the subject, *Wishes, Lies and Dreams: Teaching Children to Write Poetry*. After I had worked a while with Koch's recipes for collaborative poems, I had begun to make up poem-recipes of my own; and then I had sought ways to help people learn to make poems without the use of anything so fixed as a recipe.

Koch's recipes for poems are brilliant and simple devices for releasing the poetry in people. They provide the security of a pre-fabricated structure. They remove people's anxiety about poetry by turning the making of poems into a fun-game: each player need only provide a single line, and that one line can completely rely upon the lines which Koch has already laid down. Moreover, the line need not even be written. It may be dictated to the person conducting the workshop. Responsibility for creative autonomy is kept to a minimum.

This is not necessarily a bad thing. Responsibility in any area of our lives can only be assumed gradually. Koch's basic workshop method tends to create confidence, to free people for more difficult and hazardous work. The formulas which he devised can be depended upon to produce good and interesting results. That is their virtue. But they must be used tactfully. There is a fine line between supporting a novice and infantilizing him, and one must be sensitive and cautious not to cross it. If slavishly imitated, the advantages of Koch's poem-formulas become serious limitations. They end up stifling the person who attempts to administer them, and they hinder the growth of persons who, after a steady diet of collaborative poems produced by formula, are ready for a declaration of creative independence.

Once one has learned to work with formula-poems skillfully, they become fine tools in the poet's bag of tricks. When the old women asked me how we would make up a poem together, I said,

"By talking to each other. A poem is really a way of talking to another person, it's like having a good talk, you can only have a good talk if you feel that the other person can really understand you, then you feel free to say what's on your mind, and you suddenly find you have a lot to talk about."

"Well," asked the teacher, "what should we talk about?"

"How about dreams?" I said. "They're usually pretty interesting."

The great lady with the string of pearls wasn't crazy about the idea. She thought dreams were pure nonsense, and she had no desire to discuss pure nonsense.

The anxious woman asked me if dreams really did have a meaning. Yes. Well, then, what did they mean?

I asked her if she could remember any dream of her own that had been meaningful to her. No, she couldn't remember.

Then Mary said: "I dreamed that my husband all dressed up in his gentle voice came back to me and told me, 'Take care of yourself.'"

I and the group were stunned. My pen, which had been waiting in ambush for a good line, seized it verbatim. I copied Mary's words onto the yellow scratch pad that had been lying in front of me, and I read them back to the group. Hilda said that it was a good dream, and Mary must have had a good husband. Mary said that he was, and that the dream had eased her. She spoke of her insomnia: most nights she lay awake till three or four in the morning.

"What do you do when you can't sleep?" the teacher asked.

"I read the *New York Times*. From cover to cover."

The other women accorded Mary a marked degree of respect and sympathy. They all addressed themselves to her, drew her out, and listened to her with greater interest than they listened to anyone else in the room. She was the oldest among them, eighty-five, a woman of obvious strength and dignity. I was impressed by her, and deeply moved. I later found out that she was the president of the club.

I said that what I found beautiful in Mary's line was that her husband was "all dressed up in his gentle voice." It seemed to me such a distinguished and lovely way to be dressed.

I then asked if anyone else had a dream that she remembered. The one who had asked me to explain the meanings of dreams said that she still couldn't remember anything in particular, but something did, in fact, come back. "I dream all the time of water, always in my dream there's water—muddy water, pools—but there's always water."

She then asked me what water meant.

I said it might mean many things, that there wasn't a simple "key" to interpreting dreams.

Still, she wanted to know the meaning of water in dreams.

I said that water was often a symbol of life, and spoke briefly of several things that came to mind—flowing and standing water in Blake and Coleridge, rites of purification, baptism, transition from one place of the soul to another, "death by water." She seemed satisfied. Water meant life, and I seemed to know a thing or two about this and that, so my word could be trusted.

Hilda, who had followed all the turns of the conversation intently, now spoke up. She said that dreams were like prophecy: they could tell you what would happen in the future or what was happening now in some far-off place. Mary's dream had clearly touched off her remembering a dream of profound significance for her: "I dreamed that when I was alone in this country my parents appeared before me, and my father blessed me, and I knew it was their last time, I knew they were perished, it was just before Shavuos, 1942."

I took down her words. The moment someone started speaking of a dream, I started writing; and I left off taking dictation when the talk turned aside from the subject of the poem.

After Hilda said something more about her parents, who perished in a Nazi concentration camp, I read the three lines I had gathered thus far.

The great lady was willing to concede there was something to all this fiddle-faddle; and she was certainly not going to be left out. But she made it clear that she wanted to offer a corrective to the questionable niceness of the other lines. She reared herself up and delivered her "beautiful lines" in a rebuking tone: "I dream about the beautiful things—the colors of nature, and music, and I see Haifa and Israel and the mountains of Switzerland." These, of course, are the only words in the collaborative poem that approach being pure nonsense. What was clear was that she feared her actual dreams and wished to dream beautiful ones. She had admitted earlier that she thought too much delving into these things could make you crazy. So naturally, I had not pushed her, and I received her lines as they were intended to be taken—as a gift of beauty. It was a lot, considering her initial resistance, for her to have contributed a line at all. And I welcomed her contribution—even if it was a fake one.

Whether by accident or not, the pattern of a distinct and strongly-felt dream following an obtuse one continued. The one whose name and face I no longer remember said, "I dreamed when I was sleeping at a window near the fire-escape a hand came and choked me, and in the morning I saw the watch was there and I knew no one had come."

Hilda asked the woman how she had felt after this nightmare, and she answered, "Glad to be alive."

The dead had appeared in Hilda's and Mary's dreams, to give news of death and a gift for survival. Then the hand of death itself had come into the poem, and choked the speaker. The woman's death had approached her, forced her into waking up to her mortality, and left her intact. This dream, she told us, had occurred when she was fifteen, and she had remembered it vividly all her life. She spoke of her relief when in the daylight she saw that "the watch," time itself, was still there for her; and death, the thief who steals all our watches, had not come for her after all.

The teacher, who had thus far not spoken of a dream, ended the discussion and the poem on a lighter note: "Whenever I dream of my folks, I know I have to call the rest of the family." The group laughed—and we broke up because it was noon and time for the group worker's vegetable soup.

When the group worker read the poem we had made, he was first annoyed, then distressed, and finally, after I explained a few things to him, angry.* He said that our job was to provide "recreation" for senior citizens, not therapy. I wasn't trained to handle the kinds of experiences I had let loose into the poem. The women might go home and have nightmares, they might be disturbed by all this talk about the dead and death.

I had volumes to answer him. He found it hard to listen to me. He kept interrupting me. I found it impossible to say what I wanted to say to him. He kept demanding an explanation from me, even

* See "Dreams," p. 29.

while I was talking about the poem itself and the evident satisfaction the women had experienced in making it with me. "But what is the purpose of what you are doing?" he kept insisting. "State the purpose." In my frustration, I ended up launching into an angry lecture on the principles of poetry therapy, complete with references to three scholarly essays on the subject.

My erudition, such as it is, is not one of the chief pleasures of my life, and mostly I don't make much of it. But I liked neither the man's condescension nor his attack on the poem. I was glad to be able to oppose him on his own ground—that of respectable authority. I re-experienced all the distastefulness of graduate school, where I, like so many others, had spent several years of my life accumulating knowledge simply to be able to hold my own as a person, and where too much of my intellectual life had been wasted on mere controversy. What a hurt that had been! But now, once again, I felt glad for my knowledge: it was a way of sticking up for myself. I will not repeat here what I said. You can find all that in Jack Leedy's book.* What matters is this: all that knowledge, important though it is, was a poor substitute for the real communication that did not take place.

What I had wanted to say to him was: When you say "recreation," I hear the word "re-create." If by recreation you mean something more than bingo and cards, something other than mere diversion from the commonplace realities of our lives, then I agree with you. For a senior citizens' club to have any real value, I think it must allow room for activities that have the full dignity of work. Making soup, setting the tables, the whole business side of the club, is a way of working with reality. Poetry is also a way. It is a way of taking all that we have left half-created and fearful, all that we have half-denied and left half-unfinished, of taking all our losses and using them to recreate wholeness and health and significance.

I wanted to say: Death and dying are primary concerns of old age. All our lives, the things we are interested in—sex and self-knowledge and work and death—are made shameful for us. At every stage of our lives, we are taught not to be what we are, and we end up by not allowing ourselves to be concerned in the things which

* Leedy, J. J. (ed.), *Poetry Therapy.* Philadelphia: J. B. Lippincott Company, 1969.

21

most concern us. We live stupid lives, we live with blinders on, and we die the way we have lived—in ignorance of what is happening to us. In schools and on jobs, we are screened from the knowledge of our lives. In old age homes and terminal wards, we are screened from the knowledge of our deaths.

I wanted to say: In working on the dream poem, I learned some remarkable things. I learned that the mourning-dreams of old women are truly acts of creation. The old women had unconsciously summoned a power by which they healed themselves. Their dreams had helped them accept the deaths of the people they loved. And their full acceptance of death had been a great bestower of life. Mary, whose dreaming mind dressed her husband in a gentle voice, was taking good care of herself in her dream-life. Her husband had given his O.K. for her to go on living,. and so she didn't have to feel any guilt about living as well as she could. In looking after herself, she was doing just what her husband wanted her to do. And Hilda, who had not been able to take leave of her father in the flesh, received his blessing in a dream. His death came to her companioned with love, and so it was not a thing to be feared. It was a source of great strength.

We, the young, are the ones who fear death. We fear death far more than they, who have wrestled with it, and prepared themselves to meet it. They are free of our insecurities and our pettiness. They do not waste time and breath on all the crap that we spend our days pursuing. They know they are mortal, and knowing their mortality is a strength beyond the strength of the young ones. We dream we will live forever, and so we squander ourselves stupidly, without discipline, fearfully. We rush from one thing to the next, hungry for more. We are insatiable. We are greedy. We do not know what to pick up and what to avoid because we refuse to come into the knowledge of the death that awaits us. We are angry, hurt, grief-stricken, needy, enraged, and ignorant. The old ones can cast a cold eye on all that we shrink from and run to. I know this to be true. I have seen it with my own eyes. I have seen the young and I have seen the old, and I know this to be true.

I grew up with four grandparents around me. I lived close to old age all my life. Much of what I know comes from my *zeides* and my *bubbas*.* Each one was my teacher.

---

* *zeides* and *bubbas*: grandfathers and grandmothers.

Zeide Shieh was a poet and an organizer. He carried a composition book everywhere he went, he wrote poems sitting and standing, he wrote them in the subways and in the factories. And he organized everything he could lay his hands on. He organized the leather workers in Russia and he organized them on the Lower East Side. When he was drafted into the Czar's army, he organized some Socialist pamphlets into his boots and so came all prepared for the moment when his illiterate lieutenant commanded him to teach his illiterate comrades how to read. With Marx and Engels as the primer, he organized a plot to blow up an officer's ballroom in the Revolution of 1905. The home-made bomb let out a loud *kvetch,** a few pieces of wood were badly splintered, the great hero of my childhood was caught in an hour, sentenced to be shot as soon as they could wake up the firing squad, rescued later that night by the Bund, spirited by underground railroad across half of Europe, chased by the Czar's gendarmes, stowed away at Genoa with three pounds of mozzarella cheese, which he nibbled at for the next two weeks and which he afterwards never spoke of without disgust, arrived at Ellis Island and promptly began organizing *folk shules†* to keep Yiddish culture alive in America. He wrote the texts for the classes, he turned over his factory paycheck to the teachers, his wife Bluma had to support him and his family, and he kept on doing the two things that mattered to him—writing poems and organizing things.

From Zeide Shieh I learned that life means writing poems and organizing things, and I learned to go on doing these things whether anybody paid me for them or not.

Thank God for Zeide Alter! From him I learned that as long as I'm going to do what I want to do anyway, I might as well try to get somebody else to pay me for it. Shortly after I graduated from college, he took me on a long walk, through Crotona Park, in the Bronx. He said, "You know, Zeide Shieh is an educated man, an artist, I got a lot of respect for him. He's also a little bit of a *luftmensch,‡* a man whose office is in his shoe. Now maybe you

---

* *kvetch:* groan, complaint.
† *folk shules:* Literally, "folk schools," schools where Yiddish language and culture are taught.
‡ *luftmensch:* Literally, "air-person." An impractical person, a dreamer, a person whose head is in the clouds.

also need to write poetry, and maybe you don't. But you definitely need to earn a living. If you can find a way to combine the two things, so much the better." At nineteen, I wasn't interested in so much good advice.

If Zeide Shieh was a man who frequently walked on air, Zeide Alter was a man who had both feet planted firmly on the ground—and he provided. He provided for his family, he provided for his friends, he provided for his community, and above all he provided for himself. More than anyone else I ever met, he knew how not to suffer. Is the life of poor people full of great crises? He wouldn't hear of it! Not in *his* family! It was more than bravado, more than willful deafness to the inner complaints of himself and others. It was this, and more: a simple refusal to let life be anything else but good. He not only got away with it, he flourished.

Zeide Alter was an egg-candler. He worked in the worst of times, and when his friend was sick, he worked on his job too. This was during the Depression when to miss a few days of work was to lose the job. All week long he laid aside the double-yoked eggs. And every Friday night, religiously, he brought us thirty-six double-yoked eggs, a fortune. Whatever he touched, although it was the most ordinary thing, he made fortunate. He was a barrel-chested, squat, bald man who looked like Picasso and who also liked to pose with his chest bare.

From Zeide Alter I learned how to die.

He died on a Thursday, at the age of eighty-two. Thursday was market day. All his life he had gone down to the butter and egg market, on Fulton Street. On Thursdays, after he retired at the age of seventy-seven, he did the marketing for *Shabbos.** The Thursday he died was no different. He went down and got bargains on the chickens, the prunes, the apples, the pears, the eggplants, the carrots, the peas, the milk, the cheese, the butter and the bread. He came up, unpacked the bags and folded them away. Everything was in order. He had recently given away his money to the people he loved, he had taken care of a life's work and a day's work, and he was finished. He left a refrigerator full of food for *Shabbos.*

Zeide Alter was vigorous and healthy and active and at work until the last moment of his life. Then he just died. He died without

* *Shabbos:* the Sabbath.

suffering. He died without giving up the independence that was so precious to him. He died the way a Jew in the old country died— in his own house.

It had all been carefully prepared for. He and Bubba had talked it over, the way they talked everything over, and come to an agreement. Each one had wanted to go first. This was no small matter. It couldn't be settled in a day or a week. They discussed it for a long time. Finally, he said, "Esther, you know something, you'll find a way to manage without me, but without you I'm lost." That settled it, for both of them. It was typical of Zeide Alter that he did not go ahead and die without arranging it first with Bubba Esther.

His love for her, and her love for him, is one of the most rare and precious things I have ever seen. A few months before he died, he said, "You know, I still have to keep reminding myself not to goose Bubba in public." He was earthy and gallant in the same breath. After he died, Bubba said: "If there's a Paradise, Zeide's sitting *oyven ohn*—at the head of it.* He died like a *zaddik*.† He was a *yom-tovdikker mensch*.‡ He always came home from work with a smile, he was always ready to take me out. He didn't suffer, he didn't make me suffer, he didn't go running into the hospitals after the doctors. Zeide avoided these things, he didn't want me to suffer these things. If there's a *Gan-Aiden*§—a Paradise—Zeide's sitting in the *shenster platz*.‖ He went away like a zaddik. He closed his eyes and he died—like a zaddik. Did you ever see anything like it?"

From Bubba Esther I learned one big thing: how to give. She gave us seven-course dinners and praised us in a language all her own, a language rich with shrewd folk-sayings and elaborate endearments. From her house, no one went away empty-handed, particularly her grandchildren. From her, too, I learned how to sigh and to carry on. She completed my education in the use of money.

From Bubba Bluma I learned that life is terrible to us and that all its terrors are bearable and that to bear them without being

* *oyven ohn:* at the head, in the place of honor.
† *zaddik:* the rebbe, the head of his community, a wise and holy man.
‡ *yom-tovdikker mensch:* Literally, "a holiday-person." A life-loving person.
§ *Gan-Aiden:* Paradise.
‖ *shenster platz:* the finest place, the place of honor.

a burden to ourselves and others is what gives us whatever dignity we may come to possess. She seems to me like an old woman out of Yeats: she is noble.

One by one, the men in her family died. And they died long, slow, terrible deaths. It started early. First her oldest son, then the nephew she adopted, then her middle son, and finally her husband, Yeshieh. She has been on familiar terms with death all her life, first as a young mother, and last as an old wife.

When she suffered a mysterious stroke, and we were all of us grieving, she alone was calm and clear-eyed. She told us to behave ourselves. She told us not to fear for her. She said, "I am not afraid of death." We left her sick-bed comforted, and she did what she always has done—she survived. She survived with her gaiety and intelligence all about her.

How could I say these things to my older colleague? He was anxious about entering the dark cave of the mind and getting lost there. He was afraid that once we went in and began touching all that is usually hidden, we would not be able to come back into the common light of day without some disastrous consequence. But hadn't I seen my own grandparents handle death skillfully, as if it were one of the responsibilities of their households? To them, death was a matter of great concern to the living, and they did not shun it. They could not, and they knew it. It was one of the great responsibilities of their lives, and they were never ones to shirk the tasks which life had put in their way.

I wanted to say: The dark cave that you fear is the place of life, and we enter the darkness that we may make light of it.

2

The First Poetry Group

At the first meeting of the first JASA senior citizens' club in Brooklyn, Dina Rosenfeld, my co-worker, announced that I would be holding a "poetry group" in my office. It was Dina, not I, who first used the term. She had come straight from social work school, and so everything to her was a group. The senior citizens' club was a group; it was a group that contained many little groups—a sewing group, a singing group, a Jewish studies group, a discussion group, an arts and crafts group, a women's group. So why not a poetry group?

Later, I adopted the term. It was clear to me, almost at once, that the work I was doing was different in character from the workshops I had done in the past. At first, I considered my sessions with the old people unrealized workshops—workshops with holes in the middle. But the holes seemed very interesting to me. They were occupied by living persons who weren't always so excited by the poem ideas I brought in, and who wandered off in their own direction.

Since my own inclination was to follow the flow of talk wherever it might lead, I did not have much difficulty in abandoning my idea of a model-workshop and working with the situation as it actually was. I was as much concerned in the people I was working with as

I was in the poems, and my instinct in the workshops of the past had been to allow things to develop of their own accord, with a minimum of pushing around by me.

I had never thought it proper for me to shove the poem into shape, but rather to let the shape of what we made emerge out of the process of our working together. Then, too, I had come to working with old people with something like a basic faith in the group process itself. The emphasis of the early sessions was not solely on the making of poems. It naturally came to include the growing and suffering creatures who composed the group and were the makers of the poems they spoke.

If I clearly saw that I was no longer doing workshops, it was also clear to me that what I was doing with the old people was not quite the same thing as the poetry therapy of Dr. Leedy and his colleagues. It had a great deal in common with poetry therapy, and yet it did not fall easily into that category. It was true that we spent part of each session talking to each other about the dreams, memories, thoughts and feelings that were touched off by a catalytic text, and that this was a vital part of our work. But we also studied poems as poems, and we also spent a considerable amount of time in the group dictating—and later, writing—poems.

When I realized that I was doing neither poetry workshops nor poetry therapy, I became very curious—and very interested. I began to observe the sessions with growing vigilance, and to jot down notes on what was happening among us. I knew enough just to go ahead and follow my instinct; and, equally important, to trust the group process itself. It was all right to work in the dark, feeling out the way slowly. But I was actively seeking to know more precisely what I was doing with these old people. After five months, I made an exciting discovery. I was doing poetry groups!

And they were quite definitely poetry groups. They were the place where we found the person in the poem and the poem in the person.

After Dina's announcement, three old women showed up in my office. "So," said Bella Jacobskind, "here we are." There we were—sitting in a small circle at the JASA District Office in Brooklyn, looking out onto an enormous male flexing mountainous biceps: the sign of the health spa across the street. The male's overdeveloped and Alpine musculature, zooming in through the picture window of the office, caught my eye. I wanted to laugh. There we were: three old women, a somewhat rabbinical-looking poet—and an All-American giant came maundering in. I had a funny sense of dislocation. This time, it was not accompanied with the *angst* on the floating dance floor. My eye for the incongruous now filled me with a sense of possible discovery. It was a good sign: no doubt many antithetical and rejected images would find their way into this place.

There was a long silence. The old women were eying me, with a similar sense of the incongruous. Their looks clearly asked: What are we doing here? Would you kindly tell us already? What, in God's name, is a poetry group? And I could also see them sizing me up, moving rapidly from mild dismay to provisional acceptance: And what sort of person are you—with your rings and your necklace and your long black hair? You're not one of those *mishuganeh** hippies, are you? Well, well, that's how you young people dress nowadays, and you can't be all that bad, if you're here with us.

Bella looked particularly eager. She looked like a passenger with a first class ticket, ready to go on an adventure. First stop: the land of dreams. Where else? I naturally started out with the first poem that had come from my work with the old people.

Dreams

I dreamed that my husband all dressed up
in his gentle voice came back to me
and told me: Take care of yourself.

I dream all the time of water, always
in my dream there's water—muddy water,
pools, but there's always water.

I dreamed that when I was alone in this
country my parents appeared before me,
and my father blessed me, and I knew
it was their last time, I knew they
were perished, this was just before
Shavuos, 1942.

I dream about the beautiful things—the
colors of nature, and music, and I see

* *mishuganeh:* crazy.

29

Haifa and Israel and the mountains
of Switzerland.

I dreamed when I was sleeping at a window
near the fire escape a hand came and
choked me, and in the morning I saw
the watch was there and no one had come.

Whenever I dream of my folks, I know I have
to call the rest of the family.

"Well," said Bella, "if you'll look in the Bible you'll see the story of Jacob. All night he wrestled with the angel, and he got the blessing."

Speaking of the last line, Bella said, "This is a signal, maybe she didn't call up in a long time and something is happening by her sister, her parents are giving her a reminder to keep in touch."

Vera Rosenfeld said, "I like the line about the husband. It means he was only wearing his gentle voice, he was dressed like Adam—a *nakitter*.° He was probably a handsome man, a good man. The woman is telling herself to go on, that's what it's all about, you have to go on, no matter what. This woman had a good marriage, so it was a loss, but now she has to go on, I guess her dream helped."

Hilda Glick said, "I had a dream like that, but I didn't know what it meant, and it hurt me. I didn't realize my mother was really telling me to take care of myself, my friend had to explain it to me."

It was at this point that I began taking dictation. The poem that came out, "Mourning," is what I call a "conversation poem." It is a verbatim transcript—with only transitional comments deleted—of the conversation that took place when Hilda began telling us her dream.

I dreamt about my mother after her death.
I wanted to kiss her but she pushed me away,
I was hurt.
My friend said that she didn't want me yet,
she wanted me to live.

How many years did I spend with my parents?
But I spent fifty years with my husband. And

° *Nakitter:* a naked one.

how long do you get with your children? They're
so far away.

It took me three years to come out of the
dilemma I was in.
I went to Israel and it brought me out—
the heroes of the Bible I saw before my eyes.
I suddenly lost my only sister and there
was an unveiling.*

My brother said: Here comes the sentimental one.
I said: I want to be alone now.
I sat on the family plot. There was my father,
there was my mother, there was my brother, there
was my sister, and I was the only alive person
here.
I thought: all these people were once alive,
all these people once ate and laughed and danced
and wept, and I was the only alive person here.
You know, it did me good.

For a year you mourn, and after that you
have to go on with your life, that's the Law.
The rabbi told me: If you go on crying
and mourning, there is no peace. The year is up.

The year is never up.
This morning I was going to bake some
potatoes and my sister came back to me, how she
used to brush the potatoes.
It never stops.

—Hilda Glick, Bella Jacobskind, Vera Rosenfeld

Most of the poems made by this poetry group—because it met
on Thursdays we called it The Thursday Poetry Group—came about
in this way. After I presented the catalyst-poem, the initial conversation would often circle warily about it. And then a moment of
concentration and power came, and behold! there it was—the poem,
the persons in the group speaking the poem to each other, and I, my
hands racing across my composition book, trying to catch every
word of it before it vanished. The women were usually deeply en-

* unveiling: a ceremony held within a year of the burial. The monument
is ritually "unveiled" to the family and friends of the dead one.

grossed in what they were talking about—regrets, Florida, anti-Semitism, rejecting children, wonderful or tyrannical husbands, loneliness, loss of kin, the injustice of life, the "dilemma" of death—and they would rarely take notice of the moment when I started writing. Then Vera would suddenly realize I was taking down all their words, and she would say, *"Gib a kook, er shreibt, er shreibt!"* (*"Gib a kook"* is the Yiddish equivalent for a Spanish word that will soon pass into New York City English: *"Mira! Mira!"* combines the same nuances of excitement, alarm and pleasure. Vera wasn't only saying, "Look, he's writing, he's writing," she was also saying, "Look out!") Once she had "caught me at it again," she would chuckle to herself, and go on with the discussion.

At first, they were perplexed and amused to see me acting as their faithful scribe. They thought it odd and funny that at a certain point in the group, I would grab my notebook, and become suddenly silent, invisible, just attentive. Once, in discussing this, they asked me why I wasn't more of a disciplinarian. Hilda, in particular, wanted to know why I let the "old ladies" go on and on, just as they pleased, and didn't try to keep everybody more in line.

"Let me tell you a story. Once a child was walking through a wheat field, and his father came up to him and said, 'Why are you wandering around like that? Don't you see the rows of wheat? Why can't you stay in line?' And the child answered, 'Oh, but I *am* staying in line.' He pointed to a fine line on the ground, the barely visible trail that a garter snake had made before it disappeared. The father was so accustomed to his rows of wheat that he couldn't see the line which his child was following."

This was the first of many tales I found myself making up in the group. I was a great reader of Hasidic tales, Zen parables, and the like, and much of "the teaching" that mattered to me had come by way of tales I had heard or read. My way of finding and naming the meanings of things was changing, spontaneously, without my quite realizing it. I was no longer so inclined to do as much explaining as I had done in the past, and so of necessity I had to find other ways of transmitting my thought, ways that would help people learn without imposing the jargon that worked for me. Each person had his own experience and vocabulary to work with, and each could be left to put things together for himself in a way that would be significant and valuable for him.

Vera, in interpreting the story, said that the poetry group

wasn't like a class, that everyone in it had something to learn, that everyone was a teacher, but that the great teacher was experience, and that they, the old women, had had a great deal of it, and they also had good stories to tell.

Bella reminded Hilda of the time that I had cut her off after she had cut Hilda off. No matter how many times Bella thanked me for "teaching" her "how to listen," she was always a bit sore about it. She referred to it as "the time he told me to shut up." I had said, "Why can't you listen to what Hilda is saying?" She told Hilda, playfully, "And you remember the time he told me to shut up? When he wants to keep someone in line. . ." She didn't finish the sentence. She pressed her hands against her cheeks, rocked her head to and fro, her non-verbal equivalent for: "*Oy vay!*"

I said that very often "the line" wasn't known in advance, and the only way you could find it was by keeping your eyes open and waiting, and if you were interested in finding the line it was distracting to try to keep other people inside of it. The mistake of the father in the story had been to believe that he knew what the line was, and he could only find the child's line of reasoning by watching him carefully.

I said I was interested in following the lines that they came up with. What I wanted was to get at the moment when the people in the group were truly talking to each other, and that moment could not be legislated by anybody, it could only come when we all helped create a positive situation.

"So you see," Bella said, "silence *can* be golden."

I said I thought that the group members were too disposed to addressing themselves only to me. They tended to get to the moment of truth when they forgot about classrooms and teachers and discipline and started speaking to each other. I obviously did my share of the talking. My silence was an equally important way of allowing the group to get to the moment when the poem was being spoken, the moment of high energy, deep feeling, honesty, and vivid speech: the moment when Hilda got up and started dancing and narrating her physical gladness; the moment when Bella recalled her encounter with death at the Yad V'Shem;* the moment when Lilly Palace, Bella's close friend and a newcomer to

* Yad V'shem: Literally, Garden of Names. A memorial to the victims of the Holocaust in Jerusalem.

the group, began to speak of her "crazy wisdom," of finding beauty in things that others thought ugly; the moment when Beatrice Zucker, another new member, opened up and began pouring out her bitterness and her regrets and afterwards laughed at herself— *that* moment, which each of us in the group had experienced.

All this helped me learn two important things about learning. I learned how to use story-telling as a way of transmitting experienced ideas—and in return, heard many good stories from the other persons in the group. I also began to learn the proper use of silence.

I ended up doing so much writing in the group that they ceased to feel in any way intimidated by it. It was taken for granted: they spoke, I wrote, poems got born. Working with formulas, however, still had the power to intimidate. Hilda would speak lines that were tremendously awake with life when she was spontaneously uttering the poem: it was she who had spoken of sitting among her dead, filled with that strange feeling of grief and joy that always comes when we think of dead people who were once truly alive, and we are suddenly flooded with the realization that "I am the only alive person here." Unlike many of the classics that Hilda had read in high school in the 1920's, the words that she spoke, when she was in touch with her vital experience, were "classic": they belonged to a distinct order of experience, which she spoke of with vigor and authority, and what she had to say then "teaches me the words I need for soliloquy and conversation."*

Hilda, who was so exciting when left to her own devices, would get all blocked up when we were working with a poem-device. Her authentic speech was blotted out by the one great thought that filled her head: "Now I am a poet, I am dictating the words of a poem and I must talk like a poet. Ozymandias, where are you now that I need you? And where are you, Longfellow lines of yesteryear? Oh Milton, oh Shakespeare, oh Poe, oh Thoreau! Oh where are you, Drayton, now that I need you!" She remembered having been told that Milton woke up every morning and dictated fifty lines of *Paradise Lost.* The great poets, then, worked as she was working: they, too, thought big thoughts (in big words!) and had scriveners. They were the standard she was trying to live up to. Nothing could be more clear from the bardological postures she

---

* Judah Goldin's definition of a classic in his "Introduction" to Agnon's *Days of Awe*, New York: Schocken Books, 1948.

assumed when she was "composing." She leaned back, put her fingertips to her brow, wrinkled it, drew her head up, to receive the great Light that was dove-like about to descend into her, opened her mouth, took a deep breath—and spoke garbage. Her oracular utterances composed a manual of bad poetry, which, as a matter of editorial and personal tact, I did not copy and present to her.

What I learned from Hilda, who was still carrying the scars of the vicious treatment that poetry usually gets in the hands of American educators, was that I had better steer clear of anything that would provide the group with an opportunity for pomp and circumstance. Hilda had come to the poetry group under a great misapprehension. She had genuinely enjoyed poetry as a girl, and she had expected to find Longfellow all over again. Well, she did find some of the "old favorites," the big hits of the seventeenth century. And I found, in working with her, that it was by no means necessary to avoid the "classics"—the poetry that had deadened us all to poetry. And I also learned from her, more than from anyone else, the limitations of working with formulas.

It was not long before I stopped using workshop-formulas in the Thursday Poetry Group. Certainly I wanted the poems we made to have a descernible shape, and the parallel structure of the formulas provided a simple and liberating form. But the poems arrived at by a concentration of thought and feeling, going in their own direction, were just as shapely and far more interesting. The "spontaneous utterance poems" of an individual and the "conversation poems" of the group were, certainly, free-form, but they allowed room for the play of voices and tones and textures which made up their riches. Their shapeliness came from their directness with respect to reality. They were the thing itself—experience stripped of excuses, elaborations, pretenses, false rhetorical postures, the true voice of the speaker, coming through at last.

The group developed by the making of poems, and the poems developed by the making of the group. It all happened by way of organized spontaneity. There was the flowing, and also the containing. There was the reaching out, and also the limiting. Beatrice, on her first day in the group, did not want any part of the theme which Bella proposed after we studied Milton's "When I consider how my light is spent"—the theme of "accepting my fate." Beatrice wasn't interested in accepting her fate, she was interested in bitching

35

about it. But she did not know the group well enough to start her bitching, so she just wanted to avoid the whole subject. She wanted to maintain the high moral tone with which she had walked into the room. She didn't want the group to know that she was eaten up inside by the thought of her poverty—she wasn't all *that* poor, as we later found out—and by her intense jealousy of people who had more money than she did. No one in the group pushed Beatrice to accept her fate. The other women accepted her refusal to do so, and this prepared the ground for all the wonderful spleen that came out of her later. And once she had allowed herself to be her splenetic, bitchy self, she produced what are probably the most powerful and poignant "spontaneous utterance poems" that came out of the group.*

Each person in the group set her own limits, and the group as a whole created the limits which it wished to observe. It had a sense of its own distinct identity which, at first, exceeded formulation, but it was something that was experienced by every member of the group. Each one, in the course of our working together, offered her own definition of the group, and each one defined it in a way significant to her.

When Bella sought to explain the value of the group, she spoke of its "Jewishness." Vera said it was a place to release tensions, and reminded her of therapy. Hilda saw it as her poetry class. Lilly was interested in what the group had in common with a workshop, the making of poems. Beatrice, although she never said as much, saw it as a place to perform. She performed the poems that she had written in the past, she paraded her "superiority," and she never let up long enough to get the respect she ardently craved—and warranted.

Beatrice was, truly, a woman of large gifts, but a lifetime of working in factories, and a bad marriage, had hopelessly damaged her. Beneath her contempt, her vanity, and her quick indignation there was a great and terrible hurt. What was so terribly sad was to see her put the other women off, and prevent herself from getting the recognition which her giftedness would have otherwise won for her. She was so brittle and bull-headed that she made it extremely difficult to give her the help that she needed.

There was one session where she got some of the recognition

* See "Forgetting" and "Regret" in Part Three.

that she coveted. She brought in a sheaf of poems, each one an exquisite piece of calligraphy, each one a savagely intelligent piece of wit, the earliest dated 1915, the latest dated 1954. The group received Beatrice's poems as a thing of wonder. The women passed around the black leather scrapbook in which the poems were bound as if it were a precious object. They handled it with terrific care. It was as though they were afraid to actually touch it —the yellowed pages seemed in real danger of disintegrating on contact. They marvelled at her penmanship, they were more than a little impressed with her dexterity in handling quatrains and densely patterned stanzaic forms, they asked for—and got—a lengthy reading of her poems. The accent of the reader, an old Jewish seamstress from Brooklyn, turned distinctly British, and carried vague intimations of great times, now gone, and of Edwardian lawn parties and familiar acquaintance with great lords and ladies.

Beatrice was not the only one who provided poems. The women in the group quickly began to take some responsibility for selecting the poems we worked with. I encouraged them to tell me what they wished to read and study, and said that, unless I positively couldn't stand the poem, we would use it. The only poem I ever vetoed was "Hiawatha," which Hilda suggested. But we read sonnets by Milton and Shakespeare at her request. Bella proposed *Psalms* and *Ecclesiastes,* and we read passages from both. Hilda's Milton and Bella's *Psalms* were, for each each of them, special texts —they were the sacred texts of their youths and carried rich and happy associations. The *Psalms,* generally celebrated for their curative power, had had a steady and increasing importance in Bella's life. "When my husband died and by me the world stopped, this helped bring me back. It is the greatest poetry. I keep it always next to my bed and every day I read a little of it—this is what my husband used to read to me, and now when I read it alone, I feel he is always with me."

On the day that we studied Milton, Hilda clearly felt the pride of a hostess who had succeeded in serving us a beautiful poem. She said of *her* Milton sonnet: "It's food for thought."

Lilly Palace was wild about Whitman. "My father gave me *Leaves of Grass* for my birthday and inscribed it with the most beautiful words, this was in 1945, and I always keep this book near me, I always loved Whitman, my father was a man just like Whitman, down to earth, and wise, he appreciated the beauty of nature, I follow in his footsteps. To me there is nothing more beautiful than when my husband and I go away to the country, we spend a whole afternoon wandering in the woods, talking and looking at the wild life, we lose all track of time."

We read a great deal of Whitman. One day I brought in "Hours Continuing Long, Sore and Heavy-Hearted," and after we had read and discussed it for a while, Vera asked, "I don't understand one thing. Is this his friend or his lover? It's hard to tell."

"It's both his friend and his lover. But it's hard to tell whether this person is a man or a woman, isn't it?"

That was Vera's real question.

"Does the poem give you any clues?"

Vera read the following passage aloud:

Sullen and suffering hours! (I am ashamed—
    but it is useless—I am what I am);
Hours of my torment—I wonder if other men
    have the like, out of the like feelings?
Is there even one other like me—distracted—
    his friend, his lover, lost to him?

Silence, complete silence.

I said that there was little doubt in my mind that Whitman was gay, even though some scholars disputed this. The lines seemed to be speaking of homosexual longing and of the revulsion that this aroused in him. "Whitman himself can't accept the fact that he's gay, it must have been even harder in those days. But how do you feel about this?" It was O.K. with Vera. If Whitman was gay, so were a lot of other people, and it was just one of the many ways that people were. That was an eye-opener. But what really made me wake up was Bella's response. I expected that because she came from the old country and was fiercely attached to Jewish traditions, she would disapprove of Whitman, the poem, and homosexuality. What she said was: "Everybody is boss over his own body and can do whatever he feels like." The old women were not shocked. I was. I had been walking around with considerable prejudice as to the nature of their prejudices, and I was delighted to find out I was wrong. I was particularly delighted by Bella's response. I had always been fond of Bella. Now I began to think she was wonderful.

Sometimes she wasn't so wonderful. Her need for love, for a great deal of love from me, moved me deeply. I quickly became very close with her, but I also found that she could be a terrible *nudge.** Because of her "old country" quality, because of her emotional generosity and the intensity of her passions, she reminded me of my grandmothers, and I was especially open to her, so that each time she came running to me, in one of her black moods, in her moments of dejection and rage, it would tear at me. Her love was a jealous love, and a demanding one. She was all too quick to feel rejected when I could not or would not give her the total attention she wanted. She had to become more independent of me, and I had to separate myself in a proper way from her. This took "hours continuing long, sore and heavy-hearted."

Whitman's poem gave the group a lot to work with. I said that the poem was a self-portrait that was making a strong point: it said clearly and forcefully that a person's torment comes from his own inability to accept what he is. Something clicked in Vera. She began speaking the words of the "self-portrait" poem.† She said, "If I had become a school teacher, I would never have married a man like my husband." More than that she would not, at present, say. But she opened up a subject that had been, if anything, more difficult for the women to talk about than death. She had begun to speak "of the woe that is in marriage," and we would return to this later on, and find that it was a subject of some importance to others in the group.

Whitman's poem also provided the occasion for one of Bella's most moving "arias." I suggested that we make up a poem called "Hours," and that the word "hours" act as the starting-point for each line or stanza. Here is what Bella said:

> The hour of my first day in Jerusalem, over there
>   is the Yad V'Shem, all the remainings of
>   the ovens, it's on the highest mountain in
>   Jerusalem, it's King David's tomb.
> And an Arab soldier was walking back and forth.
> And the first thing that struck me
>   a bar of soap, wrapped in the traditional colors, and
>   printed on it was *Reine Judenfetz*.‡
> The most terrible thing I saw was the sacks of

---

* *nudge:* nag, pain in the ass.
† See "Self-Portraits" in Part Three.
‡ *Reine Judenfetz:* Pure Jewfat.

ashes, and the little children's shoes
all bloody.
The horror is finished, I want to say what I
lived through that moment.
I lost my group and met an old Jew who told me:
*"Genug, tachter kind, kum ariose."**
Then our guide was running up the mountain and
when he found me, he said: *"Boruch Hashem,*†
I found you alive. If the Arab saw you
alone, you would be shot."
I broke out with a cry, it was a cry
from bitterness and pain, the pain of 2000 years
and of all the people lived through
—fire and torture.
It took a long time till that cry stopped in me.

Lilly Palace was deeply responsive to Bella's *cri de coeur*. She said, "You never let go enough. It's a sore inside you when you went through what Bella went through."

Beatrice was not impressed. She was not about to sit back and let the title of Chief Sufferer be handed to anyone else. "I lived through it too, here in America. I worked in a factory with Polish and Italian. Haters! Haters! I lived through it too!"

Beatrice was, herself, full of hatred—the hatred of having lived an unfulfilled life. From this, much venom.

Bella stood up for herself. She was capable of yielding her right of way, at many turns of the conversation, but anyone who challenged her right to feel as she did about her "Jewish experience" was headed for a collision. "It's hard to understand it unless you've been through it—the way they tore out my uncle's beard." (Her father had died fighting the Nazis in the sewers of Warsaw.)

Beatrice sneered: "Is that all *you* can remember about anti-Semitism?"

Bella: "I could write a book." She was enraged.

Lilly, always willing to sympathize with Bella, was also quick to check excesses. "Bella, you have to live in the present. You have to be a one hundred percent member of the here and now." This phrase, which Lilly used with Bella on more than one occasion,

---

* "Enough, my child, come out."
† *Boruch Hashem:* "Blessed Name," thank God.

40

always worked, it was like a charm. As soon as Lilly spoke these words, Bella relaxed. She turned to her "dear friend Lilly," took hold of her hand, and said, "Yeh, Lilly, I shouldn't aggravate myself." She was beaming with love.

Bella had had a heart attack, and whenever she got up in arms, whenever a real or unintended offense brought on an attack of tearful fury, it was enough for Lilly to say, "Bella, this isn't so good for you," and Bella, by degrees, would calm down. It was a remarkable thing to see. Lilly's sure, deft touch would transform Bella, in front of our eyes, from a hurt and enraged old woman to a mellow, warm, even chipper friend. What made the transformation more remarkable was its rapidity. A moment after she had been consumed with wrath, she would be in good spirits again.

Hilda always sat silent and withdrawn when Bella spoke of the suffering she had witnessed and experienced. Warsaw and the Yad V'Shem were alien and incomprehensible places to her. She came alive in praise of her husband. He had provided her with a comfortable life. In doing a formula-poem based on the *Psalms*, Hilda said, "Praise be my husband! I have a toe with a bone projecting, and thanks to him I could afford $90 space shoes." Beatrice couldn't stand to hear about the comfort and security that Hilda had known all her life; Hilda became sullen and defensive when she had to listen to Bella speak of "the cruelties of life," Lilly became irate when somebody—anybody—would not hear Bella out with sympathy; and Vera seemed to be able to hear and understand everyone.

I had a lot of respect for Vera. She was never one of the principals in the group's round-robin of conflict, but it was not because she avoided conflict. When anyone said something she thought mistaken or inappropriate or distorted, she would state her own thought in the matter—firmly. When Beatrice kept whining about Florida, Vera said, "To me Florida is the last stop, and I want to keep moving." Beatrice complained that Vera, who must have had a nice bank account, could afford to say that; Vera could come and go as she pleased, but she, Beatrice, was stuck. Vera promptly unstuck her, and quite forcefully demonstrated, both to Beatrice and to the group, that if Beatrice's complaints were not entirely a sham, they were also not entirely realistic, and that Beatrice could, in fact, afford "that little one-room in Florida" which she kept talking about. Two months later, as a result of the verbal slap which Vera had administered to her, Beatrice did go off and do what she dreamed of.

Vera had also challenged Bella's intolerance of the *"mishuganeh* hippies." "Here's what I say: 'Kids of today, you're smart, you're making the most of every moment, you do what you want—you have to break with your mothers."

Vera neither poured out her heart nor held things back. She was tactful, and she was blunt. She was reserved, and she was outgoing. She always seemed to know how to keep her balance. When the time came to speak, she spoke—honestly, judiciously. When it was time for silence, she kept silence—and took everything in. If she had a friend in the group, it was Hilda.

There were the "modern" women in the group. They shared a culture in common, a culture different from that of Bella, and different, too, from that of Beatrice, who was off somewhere, living between the Lower East Side and the court of the Rothschilds. Lilly Palace, like Hilda and Vera, was American-born and a high school graduate; but her intense alliance with Bella did not leave her open for friendship with them. If Lilly was particularly receptive to Bella, Vera was particularly receptive to Hilda. Beatrice wasn't particularly receptive to anybody, and the group, by and large, returned the compliment.

Vera often helped create a climate of mutual acceptance. She played a small, but decisive, role in clearing up "the difference" between Hilda and Bella. It became clear that Hilda didn't know what to do with the thought that Bella's mere presence was gradually forcing upon her—the thought that life is unfair. If the other women had accepted this as a fact of life, and had taken up some clear attitude in relation to this unpleasant reality, Hilda had managed to avoid it all her life. She had been sheltered as a girl and as a grown woman. The misfortunes of others were something that had been made all too easy for her to hide from. She could hide no longer: the group exposed her to a range of experience that shook her up. She realized that she had gotten a better deal than Bella, and it made her dislike Bella—and herself. It upset her picture of the world. What was to be made out of this new and disturbing thought?

A poem! Vera provided the way in. She said that no two lives were the same, you couldn't expect them to be the same, and that even someone who was comparatively well off also had his or her troubles.

Hilda began making peace with Bella and the injustice of life in speaking of "the difference."

1.

Each one is different: Bella talks about Zionism and God,
she talks about the cruelties of life.

My life was different: I was brought up with a golden spoon,
my husband was a good provider, I never knew want.

I had an easy time of it until my husband had a stroke.
Until he was 65 we didn't know what a doctor was.

I gave him my all, and he made a 95% recovery.

He's not the same: he lost his enthusiasm. *The New York
Times* he had to read through and through, now he has no interest
to read it.

From the man that he was he lost all his interest, there is
no interest, I am his interest, I am his life.

2.

Hilda always had soft white rolls. Let me tell you about
the bread we ate.

In 1915 the Germans came in, this was by the time of Kaiser
Wilhelm, he was a good man, he didn't harm the Jews, he tolerated,
freedom we had.

They took out all the bread, all the food, and we got back
half a pound of food each day.

Such a hunger it was terrible! We had to wait on lines a
half a day, five o'clock in the morning we had to go out.

Three or four days the bread had to lie before we could cut it,
it was so like clay.

In the bread we found glass, rope, and dirt—mice drippings!
From this we got sick, the epidemic broke out, people fell like
flies, dysentery and typhoid. What we went through!

We were hungry and sick, but we had freedom, this was by
Kaiser Wilhelm in 1915.

—Hilda Glick & Bella Jacobskind

This poem did not resolve the conflict, but it did bring it out into the open, and give it a name and a shape. It made the conflict acceptable, and, above all, it was Hilda's act of self-affirmation in the face of "the cruelties of life."

In recognizing "the difference," Hilda began to admit to the group that she had troubles of her own. She was no longer ashamed to speak of them. If anything, she felt that life had also given her burdens and responsibilities, and she felt a certain sense of pride in the value that she had for her husband. This was a far cry from Bella's or Vera's sense of their independent value as persons. It was, nonetheless, something. But her wifely pride led straight to the heart of her wifely oppression.

The picture of marital bliss she had painted for us had begun to crack. Her husband's paralysis was the first piece of bad news. Hilda had already heard Vera speak of her dissatisfaction in marriage, so that it wasn't an entirely taboo topic. The week after she told us about her husband's stroke, she came in upset. Her difficulties were far more severe than she had allowed us—and herself—to realize.

"Yes," she said, "I'm well off all right, but I'm like a well-kept slave, with a chain around my neck. I can't even go out for an hour's walk. He won't even let me do that. He lets me come here, to the poetry group, but that's *it*. And even *that* I had to plead for. I sit with him all day and every day and I get restless, I just want to go out for a walk in the park. Sometimes, in the late afternoon, I get so restless, I'm dying for a walk in the park. Is that too much to ask? And he says if I'm not back in an hour, he'll call the cops. What can I do? He keeps me locked up."

Vera nodded and smiled knowingly, but didn't say a word. Bella sat silent. Lilly was distressed. No one wanted to approach the anger and unhappiness of this "happy-go-lucky" woman, and everyone knew all too well what it was all about: the sexual jealousy, the fear masquerading as concern, the outright threats. The strong man of the house had become a sick old man, in a single stroke, and his wife had remained a youthful-looking woman with a beautiful figure. Time had wrecked the whole foundation of their marriage. Old age would never come to the all-American male on the sign across the street, but it came upon living men, and it came as a tragedy. Hilda's husband was a representative American type: a heart-attack victim who had planned on everything but growing old, a man who experienced the coming of age as a loss of status, as a form of failure, a man so used to ruling the roost that when he did not entirely get his way he was all set to call the cops. Not only because he was worried that his wife would get raped, but because he was jealous and scared of her sexuality, scared it might attract a younger and stronger man than himself. So he became a bully, he would call the cops to support his old male dominance. Old age had come into Hilda's life suddenly, and she was not prepared for it. Her husband's stroke had robbed her of a lifetime's adjustment to male supremacy.

What I said, however, was: "We're all in chains, there's a rope around everybody's neck." I got out of my chair and walked to the middle of the room. "Here's my stake, I'm attached to this stake, and we've all got a stake in life. The question I have to ask myself is this: 'How much rope have I got?'" I moved away from the imaginary stake, slowly and carefully. "I've got to find out how much rope I've got and play it for all it's worth. I've got to try things out, maybe I've got enough rope to move freely around this room." I walked slowly around the room, coming next to each person, seeing how far I could go. "My rope doesn't stretch from here to Alaska, but maybe I've got some of the rope I need already. It would be stupid to sit down next to the stake and sulk when I had enough rope to come over and pay you a visit." I went over and sat down next to her. "Hilda, take your walk in the park. If an hour's all the rope you've got right now, use it, use it for all it's worth, use the freedom you do have. Then sit down with your husband and bargain for more."

I told Hilda that I had often felt distressed when I was carrying poems inside me and I had to give birth to them wherever I happened to be, and not under the best conditions, at home, with my sharpened pencils and my typewriter and my erasers and my correction fluid and all my notes and thoughts arranged at my desk; and once they were born, they were naked and hungry and demanded attention and I was frequently called away from them for many hours at a time, sometimes whole days would pass before I could take care of them, and I could hear them speaking to me and there was nothing I could do about it, and sometimes when I came home from work I was too tired for them and I had to neglect them, and I sometimes felt great rage and frustration. I said that it had become necessary for me to learn to make the most of the free time that I did have, that over the years I had found that I had enough time to get done what I wanted to do, but I had had to learn to discipline my time and my passions and to work in patience, and from this great good had come, that I now felt less like a mother guarding her kids from wolves, and that all the things I wanted to do got done—but in due time. Whenever I became impatient, I would tell myself, "You will do it all, but in due time." And wasn't the voice that answered Milton's complaint, in the sonnet she loved, the voice of Patience?

Ah hah! That clinched it.

Starting that week, Hilda began making her own private one-hour freedom marches.

And that was the first time the poetry group helped someone change her life.

3

Natural Talk

After hearing a brief history of the first poetry group, Sam Hock, the supervisor of JASA's groupwork program, asked me: "What about the dead time, between sessions? They make sweaters and bedspreads after their sewing groups. Why not poems? Is there a way they can carry on the work by themselves?" I saw an image of Bella sitting alone at her night table, writing a poem. I deposited this fantasy in the back of my head, and let it sit there, earning interest.

The answer to Sam's question came a few weeks later, and it came unbidden, as a result of a happy sequence of inspirations. The group had left Lilly with a thing to say, and she felt the first stirrings of creative autonomy.

Lilly kept asking me for more Whitman, and the week I promised to bring in another Whitman poem, she came to the group excited, ready to be deeply touched, and to pour out one of her songs of praise. She was experiencing what Fritz Perls calls "a state of creative pre-commitment." It is a mood that is greatly celebrated in Keats' sonnets, where it is often brought on by the reading of a poem. Poetry is, generally, one of the best catalysts for poetry. And although neither Lilly nor we knew it at the time, the presence of the Whitman poem in her mind would later enable her to combine thoughts, feelings, images and phrases that had come up in the group, and to write her own poem.

The poem that we read was section 31 of *Song of Myself:*

I believe a leaf of grass is no less than the
    journey-work of the stars,
And the pismire is equally perfect, and a grain
    of sand, and the egg of a wren,
And the tree-toad is a chef-d'oevre of the highest,
And the running blackberry would adorn the parlors
    of heaven,
And the narrowest hinge in my hand puts to scorn
    all machinery,
And the cow crunching with depress'd head surpasses
    any statue,
And a mouse is miracle enough to stagger sextillions
    of infidels.

"Well, yes," said Beatrice, a trifle bored, "the beauty of nature." Reduced to a category, abstracted and "solved," the poem was trite—and unapprehended.

"Pismires—ants that carry the urinous smell of their anthills—and tree-toads and mice and depressed cows are beautiful, hunh?"

"No!" said Lilly. "He *makes* them beautiful. He *sees* it."

In trying to make them see what I meant when I talked about seeing, about being "literalists of the imagination" who could grasp the "imaginary garden" with the "real toad" inside it, I cast about the room for an object that had a commonly accepted symbolic value, found a rope looped in a slip knot, held it up, and asked them what they saw.

"A noose," said Beatrice.

"Yah. But it's also a rope with a knot in it. A piece of carton string. It's a string and a thing that makes you think of other things."

They also thought of death and the hangman, of the guillotine and injustice.

We returned to the first line of the poem.

I believe that a leaf of grass is no less than the
    journey-work of the stars. . .

What did they see now? It may seem obvious, but it took them quite a while to see what's clearly there to be seen: a leaf and the stars. Once they had visualized a leaf of grass and a starry sky, they were struck by the imaginative landscape which held such immensity and minuteness, such nearness and such distance; held them in a single balance and found them of equal weight. And they were struck once again by the connection that Whitman makes between his polymorphous life-symbol, the leaf, and the star, which, as the journeying sun, is the source of the leaf's life, and as a journeyman, the craftsman whose work—of art—is the growing leaf. The line held Whitman's faith and key-vocabulary, and "the beauty of nature" sold his long-breath line far too short. I said to Beatrice that coming to a conclusion too quickly, arriving at the end before one had travelled through the poem, concretely, and seen the sights, was like taking a train to the West Coast and sleeping through the Painted Desert.

Lilly started to speak of a friend who was blind to the streaked beauty of her garden, and Beatrice kept breaking in to say "Of course! Of course!"

"Why the 'of course' chorus?"

"Everyone knows that, I've heard it all before."

"It may all be old hat to you, but I never heard it before."

"Didn't you?" She looked at me as if I were either a liar or a fool.

"No, and I'd like to hear more about this friend."

But Bella was having an inspiring thought, and she circled her hands rapidly around each other, to make us see the cycle of life, of recurrence, which in her excitement she could barely find words for. She had sat in silence during most of the discussion of the poem, straining against the unfamiliar vocabulary. All her passion and articulateness had shrivelled up in the face of her difficulties with the English language. Now something had clicked, and she wanted her turn to speak.

We turned to listen to her, and out it came. She said that in nature, trees and flowers come back with the spring, but for us, once our lives were done, there was only unending darkness.

I was thrilled: this was pure Catullus.

Soles occidere et redire possunt;
nobis cum semel occidit brevis lux,
nox est perpetua una dormienda.*

---

* Suns may sink and rise again. But for us, once our brief light has set, there remains the sleep of one perpetual night.

49

Bella's inspiration and the pleasure which it evoked in me were cut short by the repeated cry of Beatrice's "But of course!"

"Beatrice!" I said. I was exasperated. Words failed me for a moment. Then I said, "What's *your* feeling about all of this?"

In response, Beatrice told two stories of her own, lovely "parables" both; the first about a particular morning glory in her neighborhood that had managed to grow through the wire that surrounded it, "to poke its head through"; and the second about a flower she had seen growing in an empty lot, and she had "spontaneously started to sing to it."

Lilly said, "It helps them grow, I always talk to my plants."

Beatrice continued: a boy with a dog had appeared, and seeing him, she had said, "Don't think I'm crazy to sing to this flower." "Oh no," said the boy, "I know why you do it."

During the session, I was more than ever aware of Beatrice's contemptuous tone. She had responded to the poem, to Lilly, to Bella and myself in the same way: having felt unreceived all her life, she was unreceptive. Her know-it-all attitude was a thick hide for a great wound, and it had hindered the flow of thought and feeling in the group. It was as if the tide of human connectedness had ebbed, leaving behind four islands unto themselves. The disjointedness was more apparent than real. The members of the group were having a real impact on each other, but it was difficult for us to share our responses to each other in the face of Beatrice's aggressive indifference. What struck me most forcefully was that the moment she put aside her great desire for vindication, Beatrice was charming.

The session was difficult for another reason, too. I had come into work with a bad cold. The world was being filtered through my clogged sinuses, and reception was lousy. I was exhausted. I mention this because my cold was one of those happy accidents which, by breaking up one's accustomed practice or routine, clears the ground for a new resolution. My fatigue, then, proved fortunate: it prevented me from taking dictation. I tried to, but just managed to jot down a few key words for each person. At the end of the session, I gave each one "your assignment for this week"—the idea had come to me a moment before.

I gave each one a writing assignment by giving her back her

own words, reading back to her the key phrases she had uttered, and simply stating its central idea. Then I said: "This is your material, it's what your life gave you to work with, it's the poem you discovered in today's group, it's like four yards of beautiful cloth. Take it home and see what you can make out of it."

As we stood up to leave, Lilly said she wondered how they were doing and what their report cards would be. I took a yellow piece of paper for each one, folded it in half, and enclosed inside, for each one, the following image:

Handing it to each of them, I said: "Here is your grade."

In the following session, Lilly Palace handed me the first independent piece of writing which the poetry group had fostered:

The Twilight Years

I wonder at the marvels of nature.
My plants visually perk up with new shoots when I
talk to them lovingly.
We see a life cycle in the growth of a tree.
It blooms and blossoms as though on command in the
spring time.
It showers beauty in its foliage and comforting shade.
As the seasons change and fall arrives, the leaves
change color.
Shortly thereafter, the leaves fall from the tree
and nourish the earth.
The tree is bare.
What a sad feeling this gives me.
Similarly is the cycle of life.
The baby is born & happiness reigns in the home.
Tenderness & loving care is given him.
Then the child grows into adulthood & eventually
marries & leaves the household.
An empty feeling pervades the home & his absence
makes me feel sad.
In time our loving son reaches the twilight years.

How will he face them?
Will he be lonely, will he have friends?
Will he be in good health?
Will he be drab of spirit?
Will he have reached a plateau of economic security—
or insecurity?
All of this will determine his acceptance or rejection
of the twilight years.

After Lilly read her poem, Bella said: "This is beautiful, Lilly! Beautiful words! Words of poetry!"

Marc: What does that mean for you—"words of poetry"? What kind of words are they?

Lilly: It depends. What might make poetry for Bella may not be poetry for me.

Bella: I don't think of it. The *geistigeh* comes out.*

Marc: So it's a spiritual language for you.

Bella: A-yeh. It's the language we *eingezapt in sich.*†

Lilly: There are different ways of expression. I talk with beautiful adjectives.

Marc: How did it feel for you, writing this poem?

Lilly: When I wrote it, it was flowing so quickly—you see how personal it is. The wording is just the way I felt it. It's natural talk.

---

* *geistigeh:* that which is spiritual.
† *eingezapt in sich:* absorbed into ourselves.

4

In The Field

When a caseworker went on a home visit, or when a groupworker went to one of the synagogues or community centers which housed a senior citizens' club, he was, professionally speaking, "in the field." The field in which I worked covered a lot of ground. Only a small patch, in the far left-hand corner, was set aside for poetry groups. Much of the acreage was covered with card tables. There were many rows of lunch tables there. And where there weren't tables, there were desks. The recording secretary's desk, the club treasurer's desk, my desk and the desk of my colleagues, desks full of memos and receipts and pamphlets and reports, the receptionist's desk and the community-aide's desk, and the desk of administrators, over which there flowed an abundant yield. In the field, there were workhorses, lost souls, cranks, democrats, despots, ministering angels and petty crooks. There was sickness, compassion, despair, festivity, intelligence, pettiness, flexibility, concern and bureaucracy. Without a sense of the whole field, one cannot see the forces that helped shape the narrow plot that I cultivated.

The Thursday Poetry Group lasted for four months. Many people came and went. The regulars—Bella, Vera, Hilda, Beatrice and Lilly—showed up every week. December came: Vera and Hilda flew south—permanently. Beatrice was planning to follow them in a few weeks. And I, too, would soon have to be leaving them. Bella and Lilly were distressed. They wanted to continue working with me. I assured them that something would be worked out. This made the last few sessions autumnal. I did not open the group to new members. I simply let it wither away. I had to. Along with the winter, my fourth club had come in.

The terms of JASA's contract with the Human Resources Administration (HRA) required each groupworker to have four clubs a week. I already had three. The first club to which I had been assigned was a thirty-year-old pinochle-obsessed club that met in a community center in Bensonhurst. It was afflicted with all the ailments that typically beset an old, well-established and poorly run club. Its members were passive, it had no program and no staff, its president was overburdened, anxious, generous, stingy, concerned— and too much disposed to one-man rule. He was basically a decent man, and in a better situation he would have done a lot better; but deprived of the colleagueship that he needed, he subjected the club to his shifting moods, and the air was filled with everyone's justified complaints.

The Bensonhurst Club was like an old man crippled by the sheer multitude of his minor complaints: it could barely move without the creaking of old bones. The president complained that no one helped him, the members complained that he was a dictator, the president worked even harder for the members, the members only resented him more, and so it went round and round, everyone running laps in a vicious circle. Everything hurt, everything grated, everything became a cause for grievance, blame and hysteria. Petty thefts of rolls, hunger for recognition, stinginess feeding on itself and growing stingier, mutual fear and mutual resentment—and the disbursement of the rage and spite of a lifetime at the gambling tables. No one to help in the kitchen, no one to sit down and hear sad tales of the loss of children, no one to clean up afterwards. No one interested in the film, no one interested in the speaker, no one interested in shelling out $2.50 for the theatre party, everyone willing to lose twice that sum at the card tables. God protect any old man or woman who wandered through those portals without a membership card! The non-member would be left to wander, depressed and bewildered, before an impenetrable phalanx of card tables, and if he did not have the good grace to wander out again, a loud barking would issue forth from the keepers of the door, and the stray would be frightened off.

What to do in this situation? The club had hardened over many years into its present malformations. Committees evaporated as soon as they were formed, activities dissolved on contact, program supplies disappeared, entertainment was disrupted by the implacable rattling of nickels and dimes, and expired in a locust-like din of small change. All attempts to restructure the situation failed, doomed by an infestation of jacks and kings.

I was not opposed to card-playing. It was, if anything, a good and exciting arena to play out old conflicts and alliances. But I wanted to make a clearing for something else. I did not want the club to stake its entire resources on a game of cards.

The members played cards feverishly, desperately, as if their lives depended on it. And so they did. The card tables were the life-boats their culture had thrown out to them, after the shipwreck of turning sixty-five. Each table was adrift and floating in one of those enormous rooms to which America consigns active old age. There was room for only four in a boat, and woe unto any other survivor who tried to climb on.

In their little boats, the old people fought out their last great battles, they had their final flings, their passions reduced to holding the queen of diamonds triumphantly in their hands, or spoiling their neighbors' conquest with a fortunate spade. They were passionate in their cards because they had found themselves without any other vehicle for the life within them, and as they clung to life, so they clung to their card tables. They started playing the moment they arrived, and they did not stop until late in the afternoon. The only distraction they would suffer gladly was the free lunch. They ran from the card table to the lunch table and back to the card table with the same terrible ferocity. Sometimes, an old man or woman was knocked down in the stampede. Nothing anyone said or did could stop their flight. It would have been a nightmare, if it had not become a custom.

In the afternoons, I held a poetry group for the six or seven women who were looking for something that could not be found at any card table. It never developed into a cohesive mutually supportive group. The flight of stairs that separated the women from the poetry group often proved too formidable an obstacle for them.

Then they sat at the door, in a small circle, chatting with each other, and complaining. "Why can't we have a singer, or a film, or a theatre party?" It was a rhetorical question: they knew the answer. The card players had a low tolerance for anything that threatened their addiction.

Once I tried holding the poetry group downstairs, but the bickering, the barking, the barging in and the incessant rattle of nickels and dimes drowned out the individual voice. From then on, I met with whomever could summon up the energy to mount the stairs to Poetry.

On the margins of the card tables, sitting alone next to the wall, or in groups of twos and threes, were the misfits: the ones who were so old they had survived all their friends, the card players of twenty years ago; the old woman who lived next door to the Mafia and who could find no shelter anywhere in the world; the one who spent all her days trying to track down her son, who had walked out the door ten years ago, in a fit of anger, and had never been heard from again; the old man who wanted to go to Florida to see his grandchildren before he died, but whose wife wouldn't let him. These men and women were ignored, or worse, by the others. I sat with them, in whatever quiet corner I could find, and I listened to them.

I heard: "Last night they were lifting big tables and dropping them all night, to keep me up, the super is in on it, they want to drive me crazy, what can I do? I can't go to sleep, they're just waiting for me to go to sleep, they killed my brother, they poisoned him in a black car, they follow me everywhere I go, when I went to the mountains, they were riding after me, in a big black car, what can I do? I can't get away from them, the Chinese laundry-man is in on it, he's measuring my sizes, they've got spies in this room, they can buy off anyone, they see me talking to you right now, what can I do? I lie in bed all night and I pretend I'm asleep, I can't sleep in my own bed, they've got it wired for sound, I got a cot in the living room, and I pretend all night, and then in the morning I get up and have some tea. What can I do? Can anyone help me? Do you believe me?"

"Yes. I believe you are suffering something terrible."

She started to cry. "My sister doesn't believe me, and over here, I can't breathe a word, no one believes me. You believe me?"

"Yes."

"Can anyone help me? Can you help me?"

"The Mafia is very powerful, but now you're part of JASA, and JASA also has a lot of power. We won't abandon you."

Week after week, she told me of her torment, and week after week, I believed her. On occasion, she slept a bit easier, but the campaign against her never rested for long.

Once I persuaded one of the disturbed ones to come up to the poetry group, and I heard the latest episode of a story that I knew quite well. It was the story of the woman with the missing son.

Fanny said: "This week I got an idea I'd write Senator Javits. Do you think it's a good idea to try Senator Javits? Representative Carey did everything he could to help me, you know my case, but these ladies don't know what I've been through. The Social Security wouldn't tell me where my son is, they wouldn't even forward my letter, Representative Carey went all the way to the top, and they wouldn't make an exception. All I want is to get a message from my son, I just want to find out if he's O.K., that's all I want, just to get a postcard from my son with six words, 'Hello Mama, I'm fine, Love, Bernie,' but they wouldn't forward my letter. Do you think I should hire a private detective? How much do you think that would cost? I think my son is in Los Angeles, he always talked about Los Angeles, but Los Angeles is a big country."

The old man who wanted to go to Florida said: "It's no good that a son should live with strange people. You tell him: you come back, my son. Advertise."

One of the women in the group said, "Can't you see he's never coming back?"

The old man put his hands over his ears, and he said: "Ladies, I want each of you to give me a penny."

The women fished in their handbags—all except Fanny. She sat there impassively, as if she had been placed on "hold."

"How about a dime?" said Lillian.

"No, no, only pennies."

Abe was the licensed fool of the club, and when he wasn't being insulted, he was being indulged. He went from one woman to the next, and each one handed him a penny. Fanny reacted as if she had just stumbled upon another insane but acceptable social obligation. The other women had either been irritated or had enjoyed giving Abe what he asked for. Fanny, when he came to her, dutifully opened her purse and gave him a penny, as if she were tipping a doorman or buying a token.

"Thank you," Abe said. "You are good kind ladies. This isn't for me, I got plenty."

He walked to the door, came back and cried out: "You are the mother!"

He started to leave a second time, returned and, shaking his fist, he said: "You are an A number one great lady."

He started to leave a third time, turned back, and one of the women said: *"Gay shoyn, gay!"**

He opened his mouth, shook his fist, no words came out—and he left.

Fanny continued speaking: "Do you think I should write to Senator Javits?"

Yes, I thought she might as well try.

Would I read her letter?

Yes, as I had read all her previous letters.

Would she ever see her son again?

"Fanny, neither you nor I have any control over that. But there is something you do have control over. You have to learn how to start forgiving yourself."

"You don't think I should write to Senator Javits."

"Yes, write the letter to Javits—and forgive yourself. You have to call off the punishment, you have to stop punishing Fanny, you don't deserve it. To me it doesn't sound like you committed any crimes."

"I just don't have the appetite to eat anymore."

"I know it. Make yourself eat. That's one way you can start forgiving Fanny."

"But I start having all my bad thoughts."

"What do the bad thoughts say?"

"I shouldn't have nagged Bernie about taking a job. He was holding out for a ten-thousand-dollar job. I said, 'Bernie, be sensible, those kinds of jobs you'll get later on, you don't start off at the top, it's not good to keep turning down jobs.' He turned everything down, he was doing nothing, and he needed the money."

* *Gay shoyn, gay:* Go already, go!

"When the nagging thoughts start in, what do you answer back?"

"What's there to say?"

"O.K., I'll be you, and you be the nagging thoughts. Go on, accuse me."

"You shouldn't have nagged Bernie like that."

"I did everything I could to help my son."

"You should never have sent him to live with your sister, she turned his mind against you."

"I didn't know what else to do. My husband always used to beat him up, they were always fighting, and my sister had such a comfortable home. It is sad things worked out the way they did, but I was trying to do the best I could for my son, I was a good mother."

Fanny looked at me—in amazement.

"Fanny, why don't you try answering back the nag? The nag is hurting you, you can't use it."

"I'm not sure what to say."

I wrote three lines on a piece of paper, and handed them to her. Pretending that one of the women in the group was her mirror, she said:

"Fanny, you did everything you could for your son.

"Fanny, you were a good mother.

"Fanny, I forgive you."

When she finished saying those lines, she sat there—her face was lit up. It was the first time I had seen her smiling. I told her these were lines she could use against the nag, and if she started feeling troubled by her bad thoughts before eating, she should try saying those lines, see how they felt, and then she should make herself eat. For a while, this seemed to help. But nothing, finally, could take the place of the six words of forgiveness that she wanted to hear from her son.

Every week, when I came into the club, Abe grabbed me. And he grabbed me any way he could—by the arm, the shoulder, the hair, the neck. He appeared to be a frail old man, he was ninety years old, but when Abe grabbed me, it hurt. His hands closed on me like a vise—the strength in them was astonishing.

"Find somebody who'll go with me to Florida."

"I made that announcement last week, and no one wants to go to Florida right now."

Suddenly, it occurred to me that Abe might be seeking something more than a companion for a two-week vacation. I asked him why he wanted to go to Florida.

"To see my grandchildren before I die."

"What's holding you back?"

"My wife, she doesn't want me to go alone."

Abe told me he had found out about an inexpensive hotel near the Greyhound Bus Terminal, and he had arranged for his grandchildren to come and pick him up there on a moment's notice. He had already made all the preparations. All he needed were directions from Bensonhurst to the Port Authority Building—and a note to his wife. The note read: "Dear Mrs. Markowitz, Abe worked out all the details of the trip with me, and he will be well taken care of." It was no lie. I helped him make the final arrangements, and he could be counted on to take excellent care of himself. He made most of the arrangements himself, and most of the help I gave was contained in two words: "Do it."

"Good," he said. "It's settled. I'm leaving tomorrow."

The Abes and the Fannys of Bensonhurst needed, and got, much of my time. The card players, of course, managed quite well without me. Aside from my work with those who were too old, too "refined" or too disturbed to hold their own at the card tables, my chief occupation in Bensonhurst was paying the grocery bills and making sure the HRA forms were properly filled out.

My two other clubs had an entirely different character. JASA was directly responsible for the creation of the Tuesday Club, which met at the District Office, and the Young Israel Club, which met on Wednesdays in a synagogue in the Flatbush section of Brooklyn. I had not been sent in to "take over" an old club that wanted to cash in on JASA's free lunch program, but rather to create new clubs in communities where there had been few or no services for senior citizens. In these situations, it was possible to foster the development of self-governing, self-sustaining tribes of old people. The members of the clubs organized by JASA tended to become invaluable helps to each other. Despite the usual amount of greed and pettiness, the tone of these clubs was one of mutual concern, and so it was not difficult to accomplish a great deal. There were programs, committees, and activities of all kinds; and there were poetry groups. In both the Tuesday Club and the Young Israel Club, the poetry group became a vital and ongoing part of the life of the club.

The Thursday Club at the District Office had been organized by Dina Rosenfeld. That I was there, with 'idle time" on my hands, was deemed a temporary luxury. That I had used the time to conduct a poetry group was all to the good, but it did not help JASA rack up the big statistics. JASA had been funded by HRA to organize thirty-eight clubs, and to serve 3800 free lunches a week. Consequently, I had to terminate the poetry group in order to service fifty-five more card players with their choice of Hawaiian salad or gefilte fish. The fourth club to which I was assigned had met in a synagogue for several years—without a program, without a staff, with nothing but an overburdened president, and with cards. It was Bensonhurst all over again—but worse.

This club was torn apart by intense and bitter political rivalries. The president was a pious old workhorse whom "the upstairs" —the Trustees of the synagogue—had given the keys to the downstairs ballroom. The keys were a mandate: "Go, and open up a senior citizens' club in this place." Naturally, the man who had found favor in the eyes of the powers upstairs was elected president of the club, and the office could not have fallen on an unlikelier candidate. He was simply an old man who could be counted on to come to pray and to clean up after everyone else. He was a simple, God-fearing man, and the presidency was a great burden for him and for the club. He grew jealous of his power. He became a bully. He threw temper tantrums when he did not get "the respect." The members sat at the card tables in a state of enraged and vindictive paralysis. They did not dare vote against him. He was, after all, the man with the keys to the synagogue, the chosen one of "the upstairs." Any dispute could be cut short by invoking that magical phrase. "The upstairs," for all the members, summoned up a vague image of powerful, nameless and frowning presences, whom they were debarred from ever seeing, and with whom only their president could ever come into contact. Whenever the president saw something he didn't like, he began to shout: "Look out, I'm warning you, the day is coming! The upstairs is going to close down the club. Yesterday, Janow pulled me aside and he said, 'Moskowitz, if this keeps up, we're going to have to close down the club.'" Did somebody forget to empty out the ash-tray? "I'm telling you, this could be the end of the club." Did an unchaste word escape from a gambler's lips? "It's not going to go on like this, this could close down the club." Did someone beg to differ with the president? "Janow told me, 'Look, Moskowitz, if they're not going to give you the respect, the club can't go on. Moskowitz, we gave you the keys, and we're holding you responsible for what goes on down there, but if they won't co-operate with you, we just can't have it anymore.' 'Mr. Janow,' I told him, 'give the keys to somebody else, I wouldn't be the president anymore, they just don't give me the respect.' 'No, we're not giving the keys to anyone else. Either they're going to learn to behave, or it's out on the street.' I'm telling you, the day is coming!" This is what in presidential campaigns is called "The Speech." Year after year, it got Moskowitz re-elected. And with every passing year, the members felt more oppressed, and he felt increasingly angry and abused. I felt I had walked into the middle of the longest running family squabble in history.

After working with the club for more than a year, I managed to widen the margin of good will from a razor-sharp line to a one-foot lane. This path-making was not accomplished without violence. There were many battles and grotesqueries. Once a dwarfish man, insulted beyond his limit, attacked a three-hundred-pound ex-truckdriver with a steel chair and bloodied his mouth. Everybody sprang up from the card tables and got into the act. Both men were ready for murder. It took fifteen men to hold them apart, and it provided another huge dose of spleen for the club to run on. For a while, the club seemed to thrive on spleen.

These battles were only in the interest of the ruling junta. Dissenting members were either driven away, or driven into a further remove of silence and resentment. Everyone was always jittery and off-balance, so it was easy for the ruling triumvirate to maintain their hold on the club, despite the fact that they were universally detested. In this situation, it was necessary to become a political animal and mobilize the club's nearly extinguished potentials for democracy.

This was challenging work, and at times rewarding. Mostly, it was a pain in the ass. The screams, the yells, the arrogance, the tantrums, the self-righteousness, the hostility, the systematic disrespect that people had for each other—all of this emotional fascism left me depleted. It made me keenly feel the loss of the first poetry group. Out of a forty-hour work week, I now had, at most, only three or four hours left for poetry groups.*

The JASA groupwork program was a fertile, albeit frustrating, field in which to work. It placed a single worker among eighty or ninety people a day, and made him responsible for handling everything from the cottage cheese to the crises. It called upon him to develop small groups, but did not allocate funds for teachers and specialists. It envisioned programming of all kinds, but provided each club with only $200 a year in program money. The lack of funds had to be made good by a heavy expenditure of the groupworkers' time. Whatever equipment, services and supplies the club needed, but could not pay for, had to be gotten for free; and the groupworkers were continually engaged in a protracted search for donors and volunteers. All the considerable business of conducting the clubs allowed only a little room for intensive work with small groups and individuals. Often enough, the worker's every step was dogged by a small mob of people who wanted nothing more than five or ten minutes of his undivided attention. And this, for each of us, became the symbol of what was difficult about the program.

All our frustration and distress, and the plight of the people we worked with, was epitomized in a single moment. It was the moment when we were seized by the arm, the hand, or the wrist; seized and asked to sympathize with somebody's indignant cries about the hardness of the honey cake; while another person was standing nearby, close to tears, waiting to tell the worker that she had "to have a new hip put in," and that she was frightened of the operation; and two other persons were talking at the same time, one listing all the organizations in which he had ever held high office, the other demanding a rehash of a piece of information which had already received the routine number of repetitions and re-explanations; and the person who had played the accordion as if it were a blacksmith's bellows was impatiently waiting to be paid; and an over-bearing and forensic district attorney was demanding that this

---

* To remedy this situation, a "Proposal for a Poetry Program for the Aged" was worked out; and the two co-sponsoring agencies, JASA and Teachers & Writers, began to seek foundation support for the proposed program of poetry groups. Important contributions in designing the program were made by David Soyer, Bernard Warach, Adele Trobe, Sam Hock and Ben Kaplan of JASA; and Steve Schrader and Glenda Adams of Teachers & Writers.

groupworker, this callous fellow, show cause why his poor, old goutified mother should not be admitted into the club this instant; and a chronically irate old man was delivering his bi-monthly harangue which, purged of its excesses, simply asserted, "I rate! I rate!"; meanwhile, the gentleman who had come down to offer his services as a Hebrew teacher was about to walk out the door, and the worker was being summoned to the telephone, the sign-in desk, and the bingo table, where a river of ill-will was carrying off all the cards and chips. Throughout all of this, the groupworker was thinking of one thing, and one thing only: that he had better call for the JASA mini-bus, to take home the woman who had gotten sick.

Moments like this tend to evoke a strong and unmistakable impulse to scream, or to run away. Unfortunately, there was nothing we could do except stand there, helplessly trying to serve all these people who were pleading and scolding and yelling and cajoling and whining and grabbing for our help. This oft-recurring tragifarcical moment dramatized the disproportion between wide needs and thin services. It was the moment when the constitutional weakness of the groupwork program showed through, and it represented one of the extreme states to which the clubs were inherently predisposed—a breakdown along the dotted line.

If this scene of bitterness, strain and frustration were all, no one would have voluntarily endured it. And yet the workers were given to great fits of job gratification; and the old people came back, week after week, in great numbers. If they were angered by the shortcomings of the program, they were, in equal measure, tolerant. And more than tolerant. They could always bring an inherited shrug into play, and announce, "So when was it ever easy? Listen, things could be a lot worse, and we should be thankful for what we got." Many of them, particularly those who had grown up in Europe, were masters of the art of making do; and quite a few knew the old secret of making soup out of stones.

There were, of course, always two sides to every question. Somebody would get up and deliver a fiery speech about how the senior citizens, who had worked so hard and given so much to the country, were now getting screwed. "We gave our life-blood to the country, and what are we getting? I'm not talking now that we could be dying alone in our apartments in the middle of the night and we still couldn't get a doctor to come out, and I'm not talking about how they try to kick us out of the miserable three rooms we've been living in for the last forty years so they can get an even bigger rent increase, I'm not talking about that. But a few dollars for outings? This is asking too much, that old people should be able to go someplace nice once in a while, without being afraid of getting mugged? Why couldn't JASA get more money for outings? And why can't we meet more than once a week? And why can't we get the meeting rooms that we need?"

And somebody would answer: "And it was fun in the steerage, when we were packed in like sardines that couldn't hold down their suppers? So maybe we are a little bit crowded—at least now everyone isn't throwing up. Isn't this an improvement? And in the Depression, we had a lot of fun then too. Look, we've been having fun all our lives, so why shouldn't we enjoy our retirement?" The old irony of the *shtetl* had been given good material to work on: the JASA groupwork program was something on which it could lavish its tremendous capacity for embracing the worst.

The tributes to the club from the American-born had a very different tone: "Before I started coming here, I went to the race-track every day. It used to cost me twenty dollars a day, but I didn't care. I couldn't sit home, I couldn't sit home and do nothing, you can't watch television twenty hours a day, and it gave me some place to go and be among people, so it was worth it. But it wasn't like this. I don't have to tell you what the club is. Here, we come down, we get together, we know each other, it's like life itself." All it took was the presence of one other person, with whom this man felt in rapport, for the club to replace the racetrack. And, after he started coming regularly and became well-liked in the club, it became for him, as he told me, "like life itself." This man, whenever we went on an outing, would take me aside, and quietly slip me two ten-dollar bills—ticket money for those members who were too poor to pay. Since he insisted that his gift remain anonymous, none of the members of the club ever knew where that money came from.

The old people cherished the clubs, each according to his needs; and gave to them, each according to his ability. The clubs would not have been possible had it not been for the work of the old people themselves: and here was the strength of the program's weakness. The clubs depended on, and cultivated, the talents and skills of its members; here was a situation in which people who, by and large, had been relegated into uselessness, were not only needed, but essential. The groupworker's goal was to develop committees which would, to the greatest degree possible, function independently of him.

The presidents of the Young Israel Club and the Tuesday Club were both energetic and gifted women, and both had the colleagueship of several competent people. Therefore, the Executive Committee, in both places, was able to take charge of many of the club's activities, and to handle a great part of its financial transactions. And the Food Committee, in these clubs, quickly developed an almost complete autonomy. Each committee was blessed with a *balebatisheh* woman—a woman who was capable of undertaking large responsibilities, who enjoyed being the head of a household, and who managed the affairs of "her kitchen" with the smooth expertise acquired by a lifetime of experience.

Then, too, in both clubs there were people who not only had a special talent, but had the talent to teach it. In the Young Israel Club, there was a woman who was wonderfully wise in the ways of newts and crickets, jonquils and day lilies, milkweed, goldenrod, thistledown, elderberry, sycamore, sumac, wisteria, oak; and who was also skilled in all matters pertaining to wire, paper, tesserae, wool, needle and glue. During the summer, she would wander along a forest path with the more adventurous women, and answer all their questions with her remarkable lore. During the winter, she would come up with an interesting crafts project week after week, none of them costing more than $3 for ten persons.

In the Tuesday Club, there was an old man from Warsaw who taught painting. What made his work impressive, and more than a little heroic, was that as he stood among his "scholars," as he liked to call them, and demonstrated, say, "shading," he would draw upon some tremendous reservoir of will, and prevent his palsied hands from shaking. The moment he stopped struggling, the piece of charcoal or the brush in his hand would begin to tremble. Sometimes, he caught one of his "scholars" looking at his hands, and he would say, "Of course my hands tremble a little now, but don't mind it, you can see what I'm trying to show you." He did not hide his pain; nor did he make much of it. He plainly acknowledged his handicap, and refused to be defeated. His modest nobility, as much as the skills he taught, infused his class.

The two card-playing clubs, for all their lack of high spirit and democracy, were not entirely bleak. If there were moments of desperation, there were also moments when the clubs became wholly radiant. Once in Bensonhurst, my brother Akiva stood among the card tables; and, in his deep bass voice, sang an old Hasidic *niggun.** A few people began clapping their hands, in time with the melody of their deepest remembrance; others joined in; and, one by one, the music lifted them out of their seats, and they stood at the tables swaying their bodies, in a strange half-dance; and one by one, other voices came in, humming and singing, until the whole room was carried away by the song.

And in the second card-playing club, at the Hannukah Party, one of the women got up in front of the room, grabbed the mike, and taking a half-stride forward, throwing her free arm into the air, she belted out a couple of passionate, bawdy love-songs in Yiddish. Something broke loose. The men stood up and cheered, the women danced in the aisles; and the club, after a year of conflict, had its first real taste of pleasure—and accomplishment. After the party, the members congratulated each other on the event. They had managed, at long last, to have a good time. As a result, the club's image of itself began to change. It ceased to be a battle zone, and became a far more congenial and companionable place.

The clubs, at their best, were a celebration of the ordinary. It did not take a festival or special event to bring on a sense of festivity. A few women, chatting together at a back table, would suddenly find themselves light and engaged and gay. Two card players, sharing a common fantasy, would break out giggling. The women in the kitchen, planning a surprise menu for next week, would swear each other to secrecy—and then let a few people in on the secret. The club's president, sitting down after a meeting, would fold away his papers, and feel satisfied with a job well done. Ordinary moments, moments of contact with other people, moments of solace or horse-play or simple affections—it is out of such things that clubs were built; and the lack of funds, and the shortage of staff, could not prevent them.

** *niggun:* melody.

5

Writing and Healing

Be patient that I address you in a poem,
          there is no other
                    fit medium.
The mind
          lives there. It is uncertain,
                    can trick us and leave us
agonized. But for resources
          what can equal it?
                    There is nothing. We
should be lost
          without its wings to
                    fly off upon.
In our family we stammer unless
          half-mad
                    we come to speech at last
                    —William Carlos Williams, "To Daphne & Virginia"

During the past few years, poetry therapy programs have been
started in mental hospitals, out-patient clinics, and community
mental health centers. They have found a growing number of prac-
titioners—psychiatrists, teachers, social workers, psychotherapists,
poets—and a dedicated champion in Dr. Jack Leedy, the director

of the Poetry Therapy Center and the editor of the ground-breaking book in the field.*

Procedures in poetry therapy vary, but the contributors to Dr. Leedy's book agree on first principles. Something approaching "a method" emerges in the literature, which may be summarized as follows. The facilitator brings in a poem that has been carefully selected to correspond to the participants' inner world of fantasy and feeling, and discussion of the poem is put in the service of evoking associations, dreams, memories, responses out of the past and also responses to others in the group. It is, in short, a therapy group in which the poem is used to unlock the doors of perception and the gates of feeling. The poem becomes a means of safe passage into the darkness and back again into the light. After all, "it's only a poem we're discussing," a useful pretext which can be dropped at any time or, if that leaves one of the participants standing there too naked, buckled back on.

Naturally, in using the text as a pretext for catharsis and for promoting open, healing relationships among group members, the facilitator of the group must be relaxed, protective, secure within himself, unafraid of strong feeling, quick to grasp the inner meaning of an interpretation, keenly aware of others, and honest about his or her own responses. He must know when to intervene and when to lay off and take risks. He is there to conduct the flow of emotional traffic—to be a conductor for it, not a director of it. He will want to prevent dangerous collisions, yet he will sense when it would be inappropriate to put a stop to what may appear to be a hazardously speeding line of thought. His training will have sharpened his insight. His experience in working with people will have given him a quiet assurance that lets the participants know that they are in good hands and can let go a bit and take the risk of extending themselves in trust. He will not use the group as a place to demonstrate his intelligence or knowledge—he will not impose his insights, but help the participants to discover significance for themselves, knowing and trusting that they will find something different and better than he could have given them had he tried to play the oracle.

The poetry therapy groups described in Dr. Leedy's book do not, as a general rule, do any writing. They talk about poems; they

* *Poetry Therapy.*

do not make them. It often happens that a patient in a hospital or clinic will be stimulated to write a poem after participating in what Dr. Crootoff describes as a collaborative re-creation of the poem.* Writing is encouraged, received as the gift of healing that it is, and used for group discussion. Morris Morrison has written a moving account of a girl whose discovery of her talent for poetry was an important factor in bringing her out of a severe depression.†

Simultaneously with the development of poetry therapy in the mental health field, there have been corresponding innovations in education. The companion-book to *Poetry Therapy* is Kenneth Koch's *Wishes, Lies, and Dreams,* the book which was a source of inspiration for me and many of my colleagues. When I first read it—as an essay in *New York Review of Books,* in 1969—I was elated. I immediately thought, "Here is just what I've been looking for!" and rushed off to the group of high school drop-outs whom I was teaching in a storefront school in East Harlem and tried out the "I Wish" poem with them. That was, for me, the beginning of a new vocation, one which I was to explore with children, adolescents, adults and old people.

The two approaches, that of Koch and the poets who work with the Teachers & Writers Collaborative, and that of Dr. Leedy and the therapists and social workers who use poetry in the treatment of emotional disorders, have a great deal to learn from each other. The two fields lie adjacent to each other in the same fertile valley.

There is an important difference in emphasis: the poetry workshop is centered on the making of the poem; poetry therapy is centered on the person. What poetry therapy has to learn from the poetry workshop are methods of stimulating collaborative and individual creation—ways of making poems, right now, while the group is together, and ways of promoting individual creation as part of the emotional overflow of the group. Poetry therapy welcomes the making of the poem, where and when and however it happens, but has not ventured into facilitating the creative process. This is clearly the next step.

---

* Charles Crootoff, "Poetry Therapy for Psychoneurotics in a Mental Health Center," *Poetry Therapy,* p. 50.
† Morris Morrison, "Poetry Therapy with Disturbed Adolescents," *Poetry Therapy,* p. 88ff.

What the poetry workshop has to learn from poetry therapy are methods of facilitating the flow of blocked emotion, of creating a safe and accepting and supportive environment for the energies one wishes to tap in reaching into the rich world of wishes, dreams and lies; in translating energy back from the poem to the maker of the poem, and helping to make it part of a process of development for the growing person.

The writers' "diaries" published in the *Newsletter* of the Teachers & Writers Collaborative—they are at their best ethnographies of classroom experience—show that the poets are already interested in and aware of the personalities of the children they work with, sensitive to the conflicts that arise within a child and among the children; and poem-ideas have been generated by this kind of awareness and sensitivity.

Where the poets have made their outstanding contribution is in the development of a curriculum of "assignments"—catalytic agents—that get kids started in building their very own monsters, composing magic spells and hypnotic charms (Marc Kaminsky, Phillip Lopate), addressing fabulous creatures after making underwater or intergalactic voyages, putting together their own readers which contain "A Day Dream I Had At Night," fairy tales, trips, science fiction, exotic fables (Roger Landrum), constructing imaginary worlds complete with maps and constitutions, economies and religions and wars (Richard Lewis, Miguel Ortiz), inventing imaginary guns and bestiaries (Dick Gallup), making battlefields, terrariums, writing graffiti on strips of shelving paper, letting it all out, creating enormous murals, building monumental trees and "stand-ups"—figures rising out of their ground (Bob Sievert), mistranslating Hölderlin and Rilke and coming up with gorgeous and revealing nonsense (Lopate), making worlds in which everything dances (David Shapiro), solving "crazy math" problems and making them up first (Ron Padgett), acting out plays and then writing them down, plays which explore the kids' fear and powerlessness in the world of Big People and poems that find correspondences between what you're feeling and a color, an animal, an object, an action, a person, a place, a plant (Kaminsky), poems that promote confessional writing, poems of remembering, poems that let the anger go, poems that let the malice flow, poems that begin in associations triggered by a small object of a piece of music (Lopate), poems that give the mind a chance to run-on on its own far away from the presence of official attitudes, poems that delve into kids' obsessions with sex and excrement (Kaminsky), poems that begin with I'm Afraid, poems that say I Pretend, poems about love, loss, the here & now, matzah balls bouncing off mountains, crazy marriages (Lopate), poems in which you change places with someone you hate, speak to an America that has taken on the attributes of friend or enemy, bad luck poems, fortune cookie poems, medicine man songs, poems that warm, that persuade, that kiss, obituary poems, suicide notes, tarot readings, poems that catalogue the contents of magic bags, poems in which you imagine you're gerbel, a dog, a lamppost, disgusting menus (Pedro Pietri), eavesdropping poems, poison pen letters, cubist poems, telephone-call-to-God poems, one-word poems, sestinas, odes, alliterative poems, riddles, rankouts, bluelets (Art Berger), fake essays on weird subjects, parodies of ads, tales of apocalypse, love letters, letters to angels, Just-So stories, poems that play with words and break the bones of syntax and put gerund-splints on intransitive verbs, poems that make you four inches tall or big as a skyscraper, poems that get to the roots of words and refresh their meaning and show you not a skyscraper but a big claw scratching away at the heavens, offensive to God as the Tower of Babel, poems that catalogue every poem you can think of, without checking your notebook, to name just a few.

More important than specific formulas or poem-ideas are methods for arriving at them, the creative process by which the poet comes up with the idea, or seizes the fire that is just beginning to burn up the classroom and hands it back so that it safely gives heat and light. What this requires is vigilance and some daring, not much, but enough to take a bet on an impulse.

6

Mixing Memory and Desire

A formula poem that has produced beautiful results with children is also, I discovered, particularly good to use at the beginning of a poetry group with old people. I have done "I Remember" as a collaborative poem with thirty women as well as with individuals, writing out their own poems. One example will suffice to show the powerful emotion this formula releases:

I Remember

I remember a railroad apartment with lots of beds in Greenpoint, Brooklyn.

I remember my brothers fighting over a pillow and my father in his underwear taking care of the boys and separating them—

My mother coming in from church and my father telling her she was in heaven and he was in hell.

I remember our little dog who would lie at my brother's feet in bed and snap at anyone who came near—

My grandmother sitting by the window eating a crust of bread and saying her rosary—

My wedding which was held at my home—my mother and brother John crying—and the wonderful dinner my mother and sister cooked for us!

My leaving to go to a farm in Missouri—not having seen one before—and loving it—a new life begun!

—Anna Shaw

73

At a later stage, in connection with memory poems, the facilitator may want to bring in some of Yeats' great poems of old age, where there is much remembrance of things past and much forecasting of what is to come, and a hell of a lot of rage against "this caricature/decrepit age that has been tied to me/as to a dog's tail." No one pictures the degradation of old age more forcefully than Yeats. In "Sailing To Byzantium," the aged man is a "paltry thing,/ A tattered coat upon a stick." Walking "Among Schoolchildren," he is "a comfortable kind of old scarecrow." What makes Yeats valuable—and good to use in poetry groups with the old people—is that the poems fully recognize his rage against infirmity, but also propose a variety of "solutions." One tremendous poem about ailing memory and failing power ends:

> Those masterful images because complete
> Grew in pure mind, but out of what began?
> A mound of refuse or the sweeping of a street,
> Old kettles, old bottles, and a broken can,
> Old iron, old bones, old rags, that raving slut
> Who keeps the till. Now that my ladder's gone,
> I must lie down where all the ladders start,
> In the foul rag-and-bone shop of the heart.
>
> —"The Circus Animals' Desertion"

The poem is a magnificent restatement and enrichment of a poem called "A Coat" which Yeats had written twenty-five years earlier; there, in his desire for authenticity and directness and a chastened language he takes off his coat, embroidered with old mythologies. "For there's more enterprise/In walking naked."

The kind of enrichment that takes place when Yeats returns in old age to an earlier theme is made explicit by William Carlos Williams:

The Descent

The descent beckons
                as the ascent beckoned.
                                Memory is a kind
of accomplishment,
                a sort of renewal
                        even
an initiation, since the spaces it opens are new places
                inhabited by hordes

heretofore unrealized,
of new kinds—
    since their movements
        are towards new objectives
(even though formerly they were abandoned).

Williams' last poems—collected in *Pictures from Brueghel*—are perhaps even better to use in poetry groups with old people because he speaks greatly and tenderly and with much wisdom about old age, and about the diseases of the mind of old age, and he speaks in American English. He is a modern master of spoken speech, of the American idiom written to a measure that is at once formal and colloquial. Like Yeats, he seeks renewal in old age. Just as Yeats climbs down into the "foul rag-and-bone shop of the heart," place of discards, old times, used-up things and death, Williams also finds a kind of renewal in descent, in the decline of old age.

The accomplishment of memory is to renew old feeling, presently lost, to revive the slumbering impulse and make it fresh. The new direction of the creature, preparing itself to meet death, makes it "an initiation," or, in Anna Shaw's words, "a new life begun." The work of memory is not the calling up of old dates, places, names, but a renewal of affect, a reawakening of the moment one arrived at the farm in Missouri and loved it, a revival of the sorrows and joys of all previous leavetakings. Simply to feel the feeling, here and now, is healing.

The motto of the poetry group might be: "merely to feel the feeling is healing"—a statement which a journalist who came to observe the Thursday Poetry Group found cryptic, and which I had thought to be self-evident. When the session ended, he said, "What went wrong? There was so much opposition in the room. I was told you sat around in a circle and everyone had to say a line beginning with "I dreamed" or "I remember" or something along those lines, but this I couldn't follow. I didn't hear any poetry coming out of this."

I thought it had been a valuable and productive session in which Beatrice had begun to find a place for herself in the group, and to be taken in by the others. Beatrice's presence had been the real issue of the session.

That was the day we discussed the Milton sonnet. Bella had said, "I made friends with my loneliness"—her equivalent to Milton's blindness, and had proposed that we write about accepting

75

our fate. Beatrice was vehemently opposed to the theme of making friends with her fate. What the journalist did not see was that Beatrice's refusal was the poem!

A Refusal to Speak of My Own Life

For the unfortunate people I worry and have heartaches—
for the orphans and victims.
Never did I concentrate on myself.
I think it's selfish to worry about myself when my pain
is so little.
I laugh it off.
The animal things—the food—is here, so I laugh it off.
I worry for my people, surrounded by enemies.
Every dollar I managed I give to my Jewishness.

—Beatrice Zucker

Bella was thrilled to find a companion in Jewishness, stretched out her hand, and said, as the session ended, "I'm so happy you're here, I respect you." I had felt it would be inappropriate, at that time, to challenge Beatrice's act of denial. I felt that she would open up in her own way, at her own pace, and that a considerable amount of ground-breaking had been accomplished.

In the interview that followed the session, I spoke to the journalist about the resistance which I expected to encounter. "But where does it all lead to? What's the purpose?" I had said: "Merely to feel what you're feeling." "What does that mean?" he said irritably. I said that life was often incredibly sad and also, often enough, really pleasurable. Not to feel the pleasure or the sadness, to be numb, was all too common, and if you're feeling what is an appropriate response in a given situation—and old age can be a desperate situation—then some act of distortion is taking place inside you. To get at the feeling, whether it is rage or pleasure or sorrow, you've got to take off the blinders, you've got to get things straight and clear inside yourself, and what you get is reality, and reality is all you get.

The journalist took it all down. I was drained, a little peeved, and secretly glad about having been forced to formulate first principles. When he finished his note-taking, he looked up, quite warmly, and said, "Thanks. You know, it's my job to play the devil's advocate. And just look at what I got out of you!"

This time, I had been able to get said what I wanted to say.

7

The Process of the Poetry Group

"What's inside you it shines out of you.

—Bella Jacobskind

In working with old people, I found that there is a process which naturally synthesizes two interrelated methods of working with poems and with persons. It seemed to develop of its own accord, by my allowing the persons in the group the full play of their interests. Gradually, I became aware that, for all their bewildering variety of expression and experience, the sessions did have a fundamental structure. For the sake of clarity, I have separated the process of the poetry groups into four distinct phases, though in reality they are interfused.

Reading

The poetry group usually begins with a poetry reading, which is to say, it begins on a note of accomplishment and pleasure. The members of the group enjoy the performance aspect of reading their work.

In the Tuesday Group, when someone reads the poem he has written during the week, it is received with applause, laughter, delight—an outpouring of praise. "It's so true!" "How beautiful!" "How did you come to write this?" And occasionally: "It's like, a miracle!"

In the Thursday Group and the Young Israel Group, the reading had an entirely different character. The reason for this had to do with the origin of the poems. My presence as scribe and intermediary was a vital element in their composition. In the "spontaneous utterance poems" and the "conversation poems," I had taken down "arias," words spoken in passion, and not intended for the page, and I had typed them up verbatim, only adding the line breaks. In the collaborative poems, I had provided the poem-idea, and each member of the group had contributed a line to the poem-in-the-making. Though they were conscious of themselves as the makers of poems and often enjoyed the large sense of freedom that comes from making up a bold and imaginative line, the poem as a whole, for all my silence during its creation, was still deeply involved with my mediumship. This naturally affected the relation of the speakers to the poem. The finished product, typed up and xeroxed, always came back to them—from my hands.

What happened, though, as the weeks passed, and week after week they received completed copies of "their poems," the words they had spoken, exactly as they had spoken them, was an important shift in attitude. First, as a result of studying their own work, they began to perceive that the words they spoke in their moments of imagination and clarity were authentically and genuinely poems. And they began to feel that they were, indeed, makers of poems to recognize them as the acts of creation they were, and to claim them. The result was that some of them started to write independently of the group.

There is a process, then, of which the poetry reading is the first part, that leads from dictation to creative independence. The last phase of the poetry group, creating the new poem, doesn't only fulfill the pattern of the individual session; it completes the work begun in the early stages of the poetry group.

Initially, all the poems are spoken in the group, and dictation is the means by which the writing gets done. But as soon as the first member has written a poem on his own and brought it into the group for a reading, something crucial has changed. This positively inspires the other members. Slowly, one by one, each one begins to take the same risk. The group must be in existence for quite a while for the shift from dictated poems to independence in writing to take place. The Thursday Group and the Young Israel Group never reached this stage; both had to be prematurely terminated. But in the Tuesday Group, which has met regularly for a year and a half, eight of the ten original members are now writing poems regularly.

For several months, in the intermediate stage between dictation and autonomy, the reading in the Tuesday Group "belonged" to the same few people—Dora, Lilly, Rose, Leah and occasionally Bella. After Florence read "Genesis," she became a frequent participant in the readings. And each time someone came into the group with his first poem, it was received as cause for celebration. The day that Sol came to the group with "Learn from One Another," he called, "Bring out the wine!" And five months later, when Ann came in with the first poem she had tried on her own, it was Sol who took notice of it: "So, Ann, this is your first, isn't it? Congratulations!"

Studying

In the initial stage of the group, we spend a great deal of time studying the poems which the members themselves have made. Gradually, they come to accept spoken speech as poetry. The unrhymed verse of Shakespeare and the cadenced but non-metric verse of the Bible help to break down prejudices as to the what constitutes poetry and what is outside the pale. Resistance is sometimes great, and the change of attitude may come slowly. Often, however, there is an immediate acceptance that poems which are neither sonnets nor written in quatrains qualify as poetry.

The Thursday Poetry Group, for example, was immediately fascinated by Williams' "El Hombre":

It's a strange courage
you give me ancient star

Shine alone in the sunrise
toward which you lend no part!

They were excited and gratified when they began to *see* the poem: to see the star as a man, an old man, some sort of tough guy, "el hombre," an outlaw perhaps; and to see the dawn-scene in which

79

the sun, with its great light, is about to overwhelm the star, which still shines on, visible and distinct. "The idea here," said Bella, "is standing up for yourself. He's getting an inspiration from this star. He's looking at the star and he's feeling like a star." The poem "Standing Up For Myself" was the verbatim interchange of Bella, Vera and Hilda which came as a result of studying this poem.

Their own poems provide excellent opportunities for five minute non-lectures on the craft of poetry; and, where it seems useful, as it seemed to be after Leah read "Words," I will concentrate our studying on some formal aspect of poetry, so that they will become conscious of what they have been doing unconsciously. Learning, when it comes in a way that seems to fit the situation, is always experienced as the crystallization of something previously known, but known just below the level of articulation. It is this kind of learning and knowing that I try to be engaged in with the group.

When the catalytic text is not by a member of the group, and it is filled with difficulties, I provide background information about the poet and the text, define difficult words and words used ambiguously, so that discussion of the text begins at the point where its surface meaning is available to everyone.

Among the texts we have studied are passages from the *Psalms*, the *I Ching, Ecclesiastes, The Teachings of Don Juan,* Eiseley's *Immense Journey,* Buber's book on the legends of the early Hasidic masters and corresponding parables in the Zen masters, and the writings of Trunga Rinpoche; Yuma and Navajo healing songs, Yiddish sweatshop poets, Shakespeare and Milton; Whitman, Williams, Wordsworth, Dickinson, Lawrence, Ignatow, Wright and Blake; Mississippi delta blues, *shtetl* folksongs, American and Yiddish proverbs; we also studied the poems which have become Part Three of this book; and, on more than one occasion, at the request of the members of the Tuesday Group, we read and studied poems from *A New House,* the book I was then working on.

Whitman was the favorite poet of the Thursday Group. He seems to be particularly good to use because his poems are a great love affair between "the real Me" and "You, whoever you are." They immediately establish an I-You relationship; their deliberate absence of finish invites the creative participation of the reader. Whether he is warning

Whoever you are holding me now in hand,
Without one thing all will be useless,
I give you fair warning before you attempt me farther,
I am not what you supposed, but far different.
For it is not for what I have put into it that I
    have written this book,
Nor is it by reading it you will acquire it,
Nor do those who know me best admire me and
    vauntingly praise me,
Nor will the candidates for my love(unless at
    most a very few) prove victorious,
Nor will my poems do good only, they will do just
    as much evil, perhaps more,
For all is useless without that which you may
    guess at many times and not hit, that which
    I hinted at;
Therefore release me and depart on your way.

or whether he is making an invitation

To You

Let us twain walk aside from the rest;
Now we are together privately, do you discard ceremony,
Come! vouchsafe to me what has yet been vouchsafed
    to none—Tell me the whole story,
Tell me what you would not tell your brother, wife,
    husband, or physician!

Whitman is always bringing the person and the poem into contact.

Contacting Themselves and Each Other

This is the heart of the poetry group, the creative center, in which impulses released by the catalytic text are let out and explored. Here is the place where the unexpected happens—and dances and quarrels and kisses and tears and poems begin.

The poetry groups offer a great wealth of materials to work with. The narratives, in Part Two, are a record of skirmishes, assaults, advances, retreats, impasses, embraces, withdrawals, a history of minor victories and defeats in the lives of people attempting to come into contact with themselves and each other. In *The Sessions,* the experience of the groups is presented in all its variety, abundance and concreteness. The present discussion attempts to lump that experience into manageable, conceptual bundles, and to state the purposes which the poetry groups seem to serve.

Catharsis. The poetry group seems to provide a safe place for the expression of powerful feeling. The feeling may be burning close to the surface of consciousness, such as Bella's rage against "Polacks"; or it may be hidden under seven veils of shame and denial, like Hilda's anger at her husband. No matter how these feelings are ultimately "interpreted"—both women have good cause to feel as they do—the group allows Bella an outlet for all the tensions subsumed under the category "Polack," and allows Hilda literally to dance out her sexual desire.

But the group does more than provide its members with a good place to dump old rage or display pent-up sexual energy. Thus Bella, with her tremendous hunger to talk about the brutality of her early years in Poland, received two months' worth of steady and unfailing support. Then the others began to grow restive, although they were still willing to give her more than her fair share of the group's time. Vera said, "Well, I don't have as much to get off my chest, but she needs to do it, so we should let her"—a concession which is, perhaps, a bit too self-congratulatory. Finally, the group had had enough, they challenged her, they didn't want her to keep going on and on about how the Polish boys tore half of her uncle's beard out. "Bella," said Lilly Palace, "that all happened a long time ago, I know you still feel it, but now you're here with us, you have to be a 100% member of the here and now." "Ah-yeh," said Bella. From Lilly, this was entirely acceptable. She dropped the subject, said there was something that had happened to her just last week, a conflict with her daughter—she started to tell the story, then checked herself: "No, I wouldn't tell it now, I shouldn't take the time."

This was the first time she had recognized the others' growing impatience with her. And the simple acknowledgement that she had heard them, and found their response acceptable, made them willing to hear her out once again. Lilly Palace urged her to tell the story. It concerned a small difference of opinion she had had with her daughter, and she was obviously distressed about it. The group listened to her with its former sympathy. When she finished speaking, she laughed, said, "There, it's out!" and leaned back, smiling, triumphant. She had gotten her hearing, after all; and she had also gotten, and found it possible to receive, feedback from the group.

On another occasion, Hilda, obviously weary of listening to Bella's tales of suffering, suddenly announced, "Would you believe that I danced this morning?" She stood up and, much to everyone's astonishment, began to imitate a burlesque queen. She kicked up her heels, lifted the hem of her dress over her knees, unzipped her dress from the back, just a bit, and pretended to wiggle out of it. Then, as she was (in fantasy) naked or semi-naked, and strutting before an audience of leering men, she imitated the catcalls of her imaginary audience and received the applause of her real one. The group was delighted by this performance; and, as Hilda narrated her mock strip-tease, I took down her every word.

Shortly after this, she stopped pretending that all was well in her marriage. She revealed that her husband had suffered a stroke, was partially paralyzed and tyrannical. It was this honesty which brought her into contact with Vera. They discovered, and shared, the secret griefs they had in common. At one point they had a good laugh together over how long they tried to be "good girls," and how foolish they had been when they both might have relished some of the innocent pleasures of being bad.

Self-Awareness. In the course of revealing their dreams, fantasies, regrets and memories, the persons in the group come to reexperience their feeling, to *feel* it fully, and to be able to identify what they feel. Finding and naming their anger towards their husbands was important to both Vera and Hilda. It helped them, finally, keep the peace which they wanted in their marriages.

Self-awareness is not only difficult to come by, it is something that, to a greater or lesser degree, we all resist. We may, to our detriment, persist in our refusals into extreme old age: it is the tragedy of Lear, who hath but slenderly known himself; and not knowing himself, he cannot tell a Goneril from a Cordelia.

Self-awareness is something that we need other people for. As Socrates and Buber have taught, knowing oneself may only be arrived at in a dialogue—the dialogue which is perhaps the essential meditation of our lives.

The saddest thing that I see in the groups is not a person's grief over some recent or past loss, and it is not the tears that are shed over failing powers: these are both natural and ultimately acceptable. They are merely sad. But the saddest thing is to see a person struggle week after week against the knowledge of who he is, the knowledge that is always trying to come home to him. People who are quick to be offended, who hold fierce opinions the way you clutch banister or cane, who give out great spurts of explanation the way a squid pours out self-concealing liquid—they are a trial for themselves and others. And they are, above all, sad.

It is painful to know yourself. Our knowledge is at best partial, and won at great expense. It is an extraordinary event when someone comes into himself, comes into knowing a portion of himself that he has abandoned or denied, and now claims as his own. Dora is adamant that "you can't teach an old horse new tricks." "Perhaps," I said, "but you can lead it to water. The rest is up to the horse." "And what if the horse turns out to be a mule?" "Then it's going to be a very thirsty animal."

No one, perhaps, has changed more than Bella. Her growing awareness of her egocentricity has made her a more tolerant person. She has become more aware of the inner life of others, even as she has brought out, and made available to the group, her own inner life. Previously quick to be hurt and enraged, to feel that an injustice was being perpetrated against her by people with "inner Polacks" hidden under their skins, she is now more willing to approach her species trustingly, and less quick to make a "pogrom" out of an unintended slight.

Florence is another person in whom the experience that several of the group members have undergone is writ large. She has learned what is probably "the one thing needful," and the most useful thing which the groups have to offer.* She has learned not to be ashamed of who she is. Despair, says Kierkegaard, is the attempt to get rid of oneself, and he says that most of us are in despair without knowing it.

At the beginning of the group, Florence let on that she "had feelings" which she thought "morbid." I was struck by the phrase she had used: it seemed to imply that people speaking American

---

* Shortly after writing this, I came across the following sentence in Nietzsche: "For one thing is needful: that a human being attain his satisfaction with himself—whether it be by this or that poetry or art; only then is a human being at all tolerable to behold."

English were large ambulatory containers which, instead of having (say) Ivory Soap, had feelings inside. There was a good deal of difference between having feelings and feeling them. "To have feelings" meant that one was in a state of self-division. And Florence was feeling that what she was feeling was so unacceptable, so shameful, that she did not dare speak of it. The group made it clear that it accepted her reticence. I let her know that I thought she had already said a mouthful.

Slowly, piecemeal, she told anecdotes—about her parents, about the death of her younger brother, about her childhood. She also revealed a rather shrewd and discerning side of herself in her response to others. But each story, each response, was followed by an anxious condemnation of herself. I got angry with her. I said, "You're always so careful with everyone else, but you're such a cruel judge of yourself. Why don't you let up?" I called her a shrew, a scold. She stuck out her tongue at me, laughed, and began actively to fight her way into some real and substantial self-acceptance.

Sol, equally reticent, watched what he called Florence's "progress" with a great deal of interest and warmth. He was full of praise for her greater openness, and he was quick to remark each time she let out a bit of the truth. He also enjoyed ribbing her about "the way you were when you came to us." And Florence was clearly pleased with Sol's banter. She was no longer being yelled at from the inside of her mouth. A man who obviously cared for her was mocking her gently, and his mixture of high regard and mockery could get through to her better than any other compound of tones, because her own temperament combined a playful spirit and a stern judge. The mutually helped friendship that developed between them was one of several that were formed in the group.

It was, in fact, Florence's "progress" that drew Sol out. She began to request a reciprocity that he became more and more willing to give her. It was a case of the doctor having to swallow his own medicine. He had been, until then, an advice-giver; and he still is. He casts up his experience in the form of a moral or ethical statement. But in his relationship to Florence, the person behind the moralizer became more evident. We learned about his relationship to "the boys I broke in" to his flower shop, and found he was, indeed, a tactful and sensitive teacher—precisely the role he had come to play in the group. We learned, too, of the eleven years he had spent taking care of his invalid wife. And gradually, the more he told us, the more the quality of his moralizing changed. The impulse from which it came, the deep desire for rapport, its half-pleading quality and yearning for acceptance, and its generous concern for others became more apparent; and he made himself more keenly felt in the group.

Sol will never be one who speaks easily and directly of his life. And yet, in his own way, at his own time, who and what he is has come through to the others. Their respect and intense appreciation of him have been the vehicles for his allowing himself to realize more fully what he thinks and feels, and for his growing ability to say it.

Awareness of Others. There can be no heightening of self-awareness without a corresponding growth in awareness of others. In becoming more aware of who I am, I am becoming more capable of being aware of who you are, and as I become more aware of who you are, I am more capable of becoming aware of who I am, how I am the same, exactly the same, and how I am different, so completely different, and I am also becoming more capable of maintaining the awareness of who I am and of who you are in a single moment: the here and now that we momentarily have in common.

I began one session of the Tuesday Group by speaking of Buber's concept of I-Thou relationships. I said that real dialogue was a form of meditation and a matter of continuous discipline. In order to practice this form of meditation, I suggested that we begin each of our statements with a name. The mere fact of speaking someone's name, of calling on someone in the group, would mean that the words we were going to say would be offered to another person, to be accepted or refused.

This simple practice helped eliminate out-of-touch monologues, anxious assaults on the flow of the dialogue, half-muttered responses, directionless verbiage. Simply by saying a name, the speaker became more conscious of a responsibility to communicate, and the conversation in the group acquired a greater degree of self-regulating clarity.

Interruptions were a matter that required some discussion. Florence, even though she felt impatient with Ann's rambling and Bella's gushing, thought it never right to interrupt. I said, "I think it's all right to say, 'Bella, I'm feeling bored with what you're saying right now,' if that's what you really feel, and if you address what you feel to Bella—and if you're prepared to take the consequences." Florence turned to Bella and said, "Well, Bella, I *am* bored." Bella, for a moment, had a look of consternation. Then she relaxed. She had not been in the group for over a year for nothing, and this was not, after all, a new issue for her. She looked at me, grinning, and said, "Florence and I—we're the best of friends." I might add that, speaking these words, she seemed delighted with herself.

The group members learned that it was perfectly all right to interrupt, when the interruption made contact with what was going on at the moment. It was also all right to speak without waiting for permission from me. Bella and Herman, the oldest and most traditional members of the group, had trouble with this. Herman, when he wanted to speak, would raise his hand; Bella would start squirming in her seat. "Don't wait to be called on, you call on someone, and say what you want to say." It required repeated practice for them to overcome their feeling of being left out and to say what was on their minds, without waiting to be rescued by me. What was not all right were stray remarks and half-uttered comments. They would be greeted with: "Who are you talking to?" Often the answer would be: "To myself." It was, the group agreed, perfectly all right to speak to yourself—but not when you were in the middle of the group.

Another awareness-promoting exercise which I used with the group came from Fritz Perls: "Make up sentences about what you are immediately aware of. Begin each sentence with 'now' or 'at this moment' or 'here and now.' "* Before doing this as a writing assignment, we sat in a circle and each one made a statement which first called on another person and then said what he or she was aware of "here and now."

The different groups I have worked with have been primarily aware of different things. The drug addicts, for example, were intensely aware of internal biological and mental events: the growling in one's stomach, the desire for a cigarette, the wish to be elsewhere, the regret about the past. The college students were more keenly aware of their physical environment: the sounds of pens and pencils scratching across the paper, writing down "I'm aware" sentences; somebody's foot flying into one's field of vision and vanish-

* See Frederick Perls, Ralph Hefferline, Paul Goodman, *Gestalt Therapy,* "Contacting the Environment," pp. 30-72.

ing again; the itch on the shoulder blade moving down the spine to the lower back. For the old people, the beeping of the car horn, the draft at the window, the shopping cart at the back of the room were mere "distractions" from the primary objects of their awareness: each other and their feelings about each other. The world they immediately made contact with was entirely filled with other people.

A great deal emerged by doing this exercise, which we repeated several times. I will offer just one example. The always-silent Rebecca made some startling revelations. First of all, she spoke. "Marc, at this moment I'm aware of how hard it is for me to say things." Rose, when her turn came, said, "Rebecca, right now I'm aware that you're smiling, you've been smiling all afternoon, and I'm delighted." Then, Rebecca: "Rose, now I feel how much I look forward to Tuesdays." Florence said, "Rebecca, for the first time I feel you're a member of this group."

After each one had spoken several more times, Rebecca said: "Marc, I once thought you didn't like old people, now I regret it."

Two months ago, Rebecca had told me that her landlord was threatening to throw her out unless she got rid of "the fire hazards" that were blocking up her house. Her JASA caseworker was helping her deal with the landlord, but she wanted my help in disposing of countless small objects she had collected over the years. She had tried selling some of her things to second-hand stores and antique shops, but she had only managed to sell a few items. She had called the Salvation Army and the Volunteers of America, but they had somehow failed to show up. What could she do? Could she offer her things for sale at the club? She was desperately poor, and the extra income would not have hurt, either. I had agreed, and each week she brought in a shopping cart full of old clothes, old books, old pots and pans, old dishes and candlesticks, old linen, old fur. She spread them out on a table in the meeting-room. I announced "a rummage sale," and nobody bought a thing. Apparently, she had felt that I had not done enough to help her sell her wares. Now, when she revealed this, I felt a sudden pang, a sudden burst of affection for her, and I told her so. I thanked her for trusting me enough to speak of what she had felt. Then Leah and Sol said they were more aware of Rebecca's presence today, and were glad of it. At long last, Rebecca was welcomed into the group.

The poems that we read helped promote experiences of this

kind. Poems have been recognized as sources of catharsis and wisdom since Aristotle wrote *The Poetics*. They are also notably empathic. Poets such as Williams, Whitman, Wordsworth, Blake, Wright—one might just as well stop here—have extended themselves empathically to the poor, the old, the wounded, the dying—to the chimney sweeps and vagrants of their societies.

The poet as "a figure of the human"—the phrase is Ignatow's—is not afraid of identifying feelings which politeness bans, and identifying with persons whom society habitually shuns. He has found ways of making large acceptances which run counter to the received opinions of his day; and where social convention does not fit what he feels and perceives, he has the temerity—it is born of necessity—to oppose his culture along the scrimmage of his choosing, and to break through and win new ground for the life that has been engaged by the "mind-forged manacles" of a given time and a given place.

Community. One of the most vital things that happens in the poetry groups is that several individuals discover that they are not alone in feeling as they do about their parents, or their children, or their husbands; that they are not alone in their fear, or their anger, or their envy; that they are not alone in their self-involvement, or their sense of loss, or their generous acts; that they are not alone. Barriers come down, and the sense of isolation gives way to a sense of community.

The groups have tended to be community-forming experiences. The Tuesday Group, in particular, has created an intense network of friendships—friendships that began in the collaborative creation of poems. Most of the members speak to each other during the week, between sessions; and on occasion, they exchange visits. When Florence moved from Flatbush to Coney Island, Rose and Leah brought "the bread and the salt" to her new apartment, and helped make her feel less estranged in her new surroundings.*

My youth plays a significant role in the poetry groups: it helps make for community between the generations. In *The Coming of Age,* Simone de Beauvoir says that, in many cultures, grandparents and grandchildren are natural allies, both of them standing

---

* The bread and the salt: It is an old Jewish custom that, when people move to a new house, their friends and relatives bring them bread and salt, that their change of place may be a prosperous one.

in conflicted relationships with the people-in-the-middle, who hold the power. The old people tend to approach me as a natural ally; and I often find myself "sitting in" for their "lost" children and grandchildren, and receiving their anger and hurt, along with their respect and affection. In relating to me, they are free to express and explore their attitudes to the young.

Even the most accepting of them, even those who are close with their children and grandchildren, feel some sense of loss. Many are enraged and despondent at having been pushed out of their children's lives. This is probably one of the greatest calamities of old age. One woman whose voice is no longer heeded, and whose presence is no longer sought after, said that she felt resigned to being neglected—but at moments a great feeling of sadness overwhelmed her. Another woman felt bitter, full of a resentment that never left her. A third, who also felt neglected, refused "to be a burden." She said, "I have my own life to live." And she added: "But sometimes the quietness starts to talk." Then, too, there are the fortunate ones, and I have heard more than one old person say, "Now it is my children and grandchildren who keep me alive."

In the Bensonhurst Group, we once spent an entire session discussing the nearly ritual moment when the Jewish mother says, "Es, tottele, es,"* and the Jewish child or grandchild, literally fed up, pushes away the plate and leaves the table. What hurt was epitomized in that brief and almost universal interchange! Three generations of stories and associated anecdotes poured out. "You can't tell them anything, they think they know it all," said Bessie Kisiloff. Bertha Treibwasser replied, "And didn't we think the same at their age?" Bertha's children and grandchildren, though busy with their own lives, found the time to take her out once in a while, and she was satisfied, and more than satisfied.

Bessie, however, was feeling intensely dissatisfied. I asked her to try to look at the situation from the children's point of view.

"How would you feel if I kept piling on more than you could take?"

"There's also a gracious way to say, 'No.'"

"And what if I wouldn't take 'no' for an answer? What if I kept insisting that you eat, even after you've reached your limit?"

* Es, tottele, es: Eat, little father, eat.

"I would say: 'It's delicious, Marc, but I just can't eat another thing.'"

"And what if you were my daughter, Bessie, and afraid of hurting my feelings?"

"I told you, I would be gracious."

"And what if you were gracious, and I get upset anyway?"

"I know what you're trying to say. All right, so the kids can't eat any more food, but just look at their clothing—sloppy dungarees, and unkempt hair, it's a disgrace. They have no self-respect, and no respect for their parents."

"The kids' clothes," said Carrie, "is not a reflection on the parents, it's just the style of today."

And Lillian added: "Styles are always changing, so what's acceptable to the kids may not be acceptable to the parents. Everything changes, that's the law of life."

"Well," said Bessie, "I'm stuck with them anyway, so I have to like it, whether I like it or not."

Making The Poem

The Formula Poems: These are poems whose composition depended upon a simple, parallel structure. The formulas—"I Remember" is an example—inspired both individual writing and collaborative creation. The difference between the written and spoken poems was not so much a matter of organization and diction, but of the degree of creative responsibility of the poems' makers.

"Gossip" is an example of a definition poem, a form which is useful in exploring charged words that emerge in the course of conversation. Another approach to definition poems is to ask each person in the group to make up "a one word poem," and then to use the charged word that ignites general interest as the base or repeat-word for the collaborative poem.

The poems of Whitman and Ginsberg, and the *Psalms* of David, which organize heterogeneous materials by means of parallelisms, offer good starting-points for formula poems. After reading one of the *Psalms*, the women in the Thursday Group made several collaborative poems whose lines began with "Praised be . . ." or "I'm thankful for . . ." or other equivalents which they came up with in speaking the poem. Ginsberg's "America" might be used as the starting point for a poem whose lines are addressed to a personified idea, or a place, or an object which awakens intense feeling.

Other formula poems which appear in this book are: "Dreams," "Let There Be Peace," "A Well Mixed Cake," "The Steam," "The Wind," "Hours," "If Poem."*

The Spontaneous Utterance Poems: Some of the best poems that came out of the poetry groups were "spontaneous utterance poems." I think of them as "arias," "songs of myself," moments of unusual clarity and verbal energy when, in Bella's words, "what's inside you it shines out of you." They came as part of the process of a person's contacting himself and others. My part in them was to see that the poem was upon us, and to write it down.

The poems that fall into this category are: "Florida Poem," "A Refusal to Speak of My Own Life," "Under the Sea," "Mermaid," "Greenhorn," "Workingman's Life," "Early Sorrows," "An Old Habit," "Regret," "My Religion," "Dancing," "The Welfare Band," "Warsaw, 1943," "Vienna, 1938," "A House in Memphis," "In Israel," "Son-in-Law," "Horsing Around," "Crazy Wisdom."

The Conversation Poems: These are the collaborative equivalents of "the spontaneous utterance poems," transcripts of whole conversations. Included in this category are poems for which my mediumship as scribe was necessary, but whose impulse came entirely from the group process itself. This is the only group of poems in which I did any editing whatsoever, and it was of an extremely limited nature: excessively redundant or irrelevant matter was omitted, that the written poem might reproduce the actual flow of the group's concentration, disencumbered of asides and hindrances.

The poems of this type are: "The Difference," "A Thing Is Going On With You Even If You Don't Welcome It," "The Boss of Words," "Signs of Death," "Images of What We Wish," "The Good Girls," "Forgetting," "Florida."

Suggestions, Starting-Points and Assignments: This category lumps together all the poems that came, directly or indirectly, from a poem idea that I offered to an individual or to the group. What I sometimes offered a person was merely validation of his or her own idea. When I recognized, for example, that an incident in the group had kindled Dora Brown's fantasy, I suggested that she go

---

* For page numbers, see "The Poems" following "Contents."

home and write about it. I merely affirmed that she did, indeed, have a story or poem in her possession; and the story that she wrote, "Jealous Husband," was all her own. The poems written independently, but at my suggestion, were: "The Twilight Years" (Palace), "Our Twilight Years" (Kitzinger), "Learn from One Another," "Genesis," "The First Fish of the Human Race," "The Beginning & The End."

The nature of my collaboration with the groups varied considerably. Sometimes I provided the starting-point for a conversation, which I then transcribed. "Dreams, Prayers and Visions" flowed out of the members of the Bensonhurst Group after I read them a healing song that I had written for my father. It is an old custom: if you want to hear someone else's stories, first tell one of your own; and my having shared a powerful and imaginative experience with the members of the group elicited from them their own visionary stories of birth, sickness and death. Other poems that "just happened" after I had provided the starting-point or suggested the key-idea were: "Mourning," "Decisions," "Hostile Territory," "Self-Portraits," "Standing Up For Myself," "Palermo, 1898," "It Was Fated," "Recovery."

The assignments which poets use in poetry workshops can, from time to time, call forth the full creativity of the persons he works with. But even where they do not put a person in touch with that vital place in himself from which the poem comes, they are useful in exercising and warming up the mind for the poem which a person may later come to write. They are, then, a form of "practice," and part of a large and essential exercise which compares the whole mind for acts of creation.

The four assignments described below show both the value and the limitations of assignments. The poems they elicited were, on the whole, less valuable than those which were born out of the internal necessity of the autonomous maker of poems, but they were, nonetheless, extremely useful in enhancing the group members' imaginative range and in developing their sensitivity to language.

The Composition of Place: The "composition of place" is part of the spiritual discipline of the Jesuits. The novice or retreatant is instructed to summon forth a concrete vision of the object of his meditation; to imagine himself in the presence of sacred events or persons; and to bring his whole soul into activity in relation to the things he has mentally composed: the imagination, the will, the understanding and the affections are to be fully engaged in a sensory experience which is, like the image-making of the poet, a discipline of the spirit. Once the "composition of place" is complete, the "colloquy" begins, and the retreatant speaks directly and intimately to the persons or angels or more divine beings who are, in imagination, standing before him.

The Jesuit method of meditation had a profound influence on English poetry in the seventeenth century; it also had a considerable impact upon a group of old Jews in Flatbush. In working with the Young Israel Group, I frequently made use of a method which was derived from St. Ignatius Loyola's *Spiritual Exercises,* and which had shaped the imaginations of such diverse poets as Donne and Hopkins and Joyce.

When we made "The Snake," I asked the group to imagine that it was in the Garden of Eden. A fertile vein was touched, and the landscape grew lush and radiant around us. Then, at my suggestion, the group transformed itself into the eloquent snake, and the whole purpose of its "colloquy" with Eve was to seduce her into eating the apple.

In "The Prophecy," the group returned once again to the first days of the world; and gifted with foreknowledge, they held their "colloquy" with the still-innocent Cain, whom they imagined sitting before them, in the chair where I sat.

The "mountain top poems" and the "airplane poems" were pure compositions of place. The members of the group imagined that, here and now, they were looking out at the earth from an unusual vantage point. A long, vertical shift in their habitual perspective helped them imaginatively grasp a large vision of things.

The "Words to a Sad Old Man" was a colloquy with an invisible presence which had been summoned into the room by William Carlos Williams. The man with the haggard beard who aroused Williams' compassion in "To a Man Dying on His Feet" stepped out of the poem, sat down on the empty chair between Ben Silverstein and Florence Novodoff, and received the group members' encouragement and advice. They found a home for him in a poem called "Shorel Manor," and they bade him rouse himself and be alive with life. They were speaking only to an imaginary person, and they were speaking directly to the depressed part of themselves which occasionally grew weary and wished merely to subside and be done with the irreversible toil of their lives.

Crazy Antonyms and Homonym Couplets: One afternoon, as I walked into the Tuesday Group, Dora and Leah were puzzling over "homonyms," "synonyms" and "antonyms." Leah had once known the meanings of these terms, but was no longer so sure of them. Dora grabbed me and said she wanted an explanation. My mind raced: how could I convert this into an assignment?

The simplicity of ingenuity of an assignment is not the measure of its worth. A good assignment is one which answers the group members' desire for growth and learning. Therefore, I welcomed any direct request for new learning, and tried to use it as the basis of an assignment.

Teaching "antonyms" was easy—and fun. I threw out a word and the group members threw back its opposite—a verbal game of catch. Then I introduced "synonyms." I threw out a word, like "squat," and called, "Synonym." Response: "Fat." I called for a second synonym. Response: "Sit." "Now, an antonym." "Stand." Then, another word: "Tender, antonym." "Violent." "Another antonym." "Hard." "And another." "Tough." "Tender, synonym." "Raw." "Another synonym." "Compassionate." And so on. The wordplay was conducted like a ping-pong match. The idea was to keep the metaphorical ball moving quickly, and to make a few smashes.

After exercising the group's verbal forehand and backhand, I thought it was time for a real game. "O.K.," I said, "now we're going to make up a 'crazy antonyms' poem. I'll give you an example of what I mean. 'The mellow hippo was necking with the frustrated giraffe.'" I made up several more examples, where the logical opposition came in the adjectives, and the free play of the imagination came in the nouns, and the whole thing was tied together with a strong verb in the middle. Then, working in groups of two and three, they collaborated on their own "crazy antonyms." Ann, Rebecca and Rose wrote the following:

The cruel man spanked the compassionate woman.
The dull eye stared at the bright sunset.
The little dog was strutting with the large
German shepherd.
The elephant and the mouse were amusing each other.
The cruise didn't compare with my visit to the moon.
After eating the sour sauce, the ice-cream made
a pleasant treat.

All the "crazy antonyms" of the group were read; the time had come to move on to homonyms. I began with a little talk: "Poets are people who are keenly aware of things," I said. "We've spent a lot of time becoming more aware of ourselves and each other, and it's also good that we spend time becoming more aware of words and the sounds of words. Homonyms are words that sound the same, but have different meanings. It's a very interesting relationship—like identical twins that have completely different personalities. Once you start being aware of homonyms, you'll find them all over the place." I took a moment to cook up some homonym-grits for them to chew over, and then read them this sentence: "The medicine man stepped on the heel of the pumpernickel with the heel of his left foot in order to heal the sick girl, but the quack did the same thing because he was a heel." I asked them how many "heels" they had heard, and then I asked them for homonyms.

Florence and Libby were prolific: homonyms poured from their lips. And all of them, no matter how many homonyms they came up with, felt an excited sense of verbal discovery. I asked them to take a few minutes and work up their own lists of homonyms. Bella found five pairs, and given the three years she had spent in night school struggling to learn English, she felt tremendous pride in those ten words. And she felt something else: that list of homonyms brought back an unexpected sense of consolation. After the death of her husband, she had gone to high school in an effort to overcome her grief, and the assignment had reminded her of her English class, and the first pain-free days of her widowhood.

The word-lists were a preliminary exercise for an assignment. I copied Libby's first two pairs of homonyms onto a blank sheet of paper in large, blue, block letters:

PAIL   SUN
SON   PALE

I said that we were going to use these four words to compose "a homonym couplet." Homonyms they knew about. But what was a couplet? Well, a couplet was two lines of poetry that worked together as a single unit of utterance, and the two lines were usually stitched together by the use of rime. We, however, were going to do our stitching with homonyms. The first line of the couplet would contain "son" and "pail"; the second, "sun" and "pale." Now, who could give us a couplet?

Libby dashed off two sentences and read them to the group: "The farmer's son took a pail to give to his friend. And he wore a large-brimmed hat to shield his pale face from the sun."

Bella was confused. But by the end of the session, after many exemplary "homonym couplets" had been made, she caught on. I asked them to go out and find more homonyms, and to compose four "homonym couplets."

They returned the following week with gigantic lists, and playful couplets. Leah's "Hoarse Meat" is representative of the writing which this assignment elicited:

> I will tell you a real tale about a little
> boy who had an imaginary friend.

> The friend was a black dog that had a curly
> tail that would go back and forth whenever it
> saw a fishing reel because the dog knew it was
> going for a walk.

> "I heard you had heavy rains here."
> "Did you hear how slippery the roads were?"
> he said, and pulled back the reins just in time.

> Sol was the sole owner of a big piece of land.
> He thought if he could build his own house
> he would have peace of soul.

> I am going to meet my sister for lunch but
> I am hoarse because I have a bad cold, so I will
> stay on a light diet.
> There is just one kind of food I wouldn't care
> to eat, and that's horse meat.

Correspondence Poems: This assignment was suggested to me by Jerome Rothenberg's translation of several brief passages from the *I Ching.** Under the title "Correspondences," he brings together passages such as this one:

> The Receptive is the earth, the mother. It is cloth, a kettle, frugality, it is level, it is a cow with a calf, a large wagon, form, the multitude, a shaft. Among the various kinds of soil, it is black.

In his "Commentaries," he says that these texts "show a developed ability to think-in-images, to place name against name, quality

---

* Jerome Rothenberg, *Technicians of the Sacred* (Garden City, N.Y., Doubleday & Company, 1968), p. 18.

against quality, while retaining the passion for the names of things which Gertrude Stein saw as the basis of all poetry. Partly it's a question of resemblances and analogy, but at this point where 'we' are, what's of still greater importance is the possibility of a kind of tension, energy, etc., generated by the joining of disparate, even arbitrary images."

Before the members of the Tuesday Group were disposed to seeing "The Receptive" as a "handy ancient manual of the poetic process," they wanted to see the kind of sense that it made, and to discover the resemblances and analogies that lay hidden in the silences, between words.

"Mother" generated the first interconnections. The cow, with its calf, was naturally analogous; and the kettle, in shape and purpose, was an equivalent of the breast: the mother, having given suck to her infant, poured tea for her guest. The earth received the spring rain, that it might bear fruit in the summer, out of its black soil, its most fertile kind; and the wagon, in which a multitude of things might be carried, was a form-holding form, a receptive vehicle. The shaft, explained Florence, was not the shaft or axle of a wagon, but an air-shaft or elevator-shaft, an empty space, a female symbol, a vagina.

"The Receptive" was itself receptive: it was full with a fullness with defined empty spaces for the contemplative mind to move in, and therefore it was capable of summoning the intelligence and the imagination of its readers, just as the chairs they sat in had invited their bodies: without a fitting empty space, neither the chair nor the poem could admit the whole person.

After we had walked awhile among the silent places, between the words, I said that the old Chinese poet had built up our experience of the Receptive by combining words that belonged to different categories of experience. In this, and the other passages, we found persons, animals, qualities, colors, objects in nature, ideas and man-made artifacts. It seemed that there was a deep correspondence between different portions of our experience, and that one of the things which poets did was to bring together fragmentary perceptions and link them in images which were, in turn, linked to other images and to a larger coherence. In this sense, the passages from the *I Ching* might be seen as "pure poetry"—the primary process of the metaphor-making mind stripped of any secondary elaborations.

I said that thinking in metaphors was something that we all did all the time, but that for the most part we did not attend to the quick flow and rapid change of images, to the dazzling stream of perceptions that perpetually ran just below the husk of our "normal" consciousness. To demonstrate that the poetic process of the *I Ching* was part of the process of their own thinking, I asked, "What color is anger?" "Red," cried Florence. "And what person is anger?" "The father!" Florence answered again. "Does anyone have any other ideas about what person anger is?" "No," said Libby, "it's the father all right." "What animal is it, then?" "A dog," said Bella. "A dragon," said Florence. Working with each of the categories which the *I Ching* proposed, the group offered a great many anger-animals, anger-objects, and so on. And so we collaboratively collected a group of words that corresponded to each other, and to the idea of anger.

In a similar manner, the group worked up several other "correspondences," starting from an idea or a feeling which a member of the group proposed. Then I asked the members of the group to work alone, to select their own starting-points, and to come up with their own correspondences. "These will be your words, the words your imagination gave you, the words which work together for you. Take them and use them in a poem. There's only one requirement: that you use *all* your words, and that you just let them come together in whatever way they seem to come together for you. Trust the correspondences that are already there between the words, and don't worry too much about trying to sound logical. Use the words and just accept whatever meaning seems to grow out of them."

They prepared their lists of corresponding words during the session; and they wrote their "correspondence poems" at home. "Emotion" and "Compassion" came out of this assignment; so did Florence's "Anger."

1.
Anger is red, it is violent, it means
a passionate storm, it has an ugly face,
it is the rage.
   It is flood and destruction, it is
advance. To the timid heart, it is terrifying.
It is fury, it is horrid.

It is a bull, it is a dragon, it is blood.
In man it lies dormant until aroused.
It is the father.

2.

The violent storm with an ugly face
caused flood and destruction, it was
terrifying in its fury.
    The bull and dragon were not subject
to a timid heart. They too were frightened
because they knew that the father can cause
blood to flow.

Association Poems: In preparing the ground for this assignment, we studied two poems by D. H. Lawrence. The first was
"Brooding Grief":

A yellow leaf, from the darkness
Hops like a frog before me;
Why do I start and stand still?

I was watching the woman who bore me
Stretched in the brindled darkness
Of the sick-room, rigid with will
To die: and the quick leaf tore me
Back to this rainy swill
Of leaves and lamps and the city street
    mingled before me.

The second was "Sorrow":

Why does the thin grey strand
Floating up from the forgotten
Cigarette between my fingers,
Why does it trouble me?

Ah, you will understand;
When I carried my mother downstairs,
A few times only, at the beginning
Of her soft-foot malady,

I should find, for a reprimand
Of my gaiety, a few long grey hairs
On the breast of my coat; and one by one
I watched them float up the dark chimney.

The primary object of our study was to trace the effect of the "yellow leaf" and the "grey strand" upon the consciousness of the poet. Both images make him "start" from the place where he is, and go to another place; they startle him, they trouble him, and, above all, they evoke a sudden intensification of feeling, and bring on a state of speculation that leads clear through to a small but important revelation.

Both poems explore the conjunction of reverie and reality. In "Brooding Grief," the two states of mind are fused together, confused: the yellow leaf comes "from the darkness" to call him back from a reverie so intense it has become the reality in which he moves, and he "awakens" to find himself in a strange place that mingles the darkness of his mother's death-bed and the darkness of the city street on which he stands. The leaf that tears him from his mother's side, although quick with life, is also yellow with decay; it is "a frog" that turns his mind away from the tortured body of his mother to "this rainy swill," this pig-wash. He has moved from one "brindled" or streaked darkness to another. After leaving his dying mother, the city street is swinish, inhospitable and grotesque.

The second poem reverses the process of the first. "Sorrow" implicitly recreates, as the necessary precondition of the poem, a previous state of equilibrium which is not the equilibrium of total attention, of reverie, but an equilibrium that is regained after death and mourning. The poem tells us that his mourning, because informed by guilt, is not nearly complete.

The "grey strand" evokes an involuntary memory which, for a moment, he cannot place. He feels a moment of disturbance, and then it all comes back in an instant—"Ah, you will understand." The smoke of the "forgotten" cigarette makes him remember one of those trivial moments of ordinary life which we do not seem to register, and which we afterwards never forget, for it has become an emblem of momentous experience. He remembers carrying his mother downstairs, to the family parlor, "a few times only"; and he sees, once again, her long grey hairs on "the breast" of his coat. In remembering how he picked them off and watched them float up the dark chimney, he re-experiences the agony of his mother's sick-room, where he watched her die a slow and terrible death. His mind turns back to the reverie of the first poem; and once again he is reprimanded for a moment of forgetfulness, of gaiety, which his passionate love for his mother and his strong guilt do not allow him to find acceptable.

After studying these poems, I asked the members of the group to find their own equivalents for Lawrence's "grey strand" and "yellow leaf," and to write poems that would fuse a concrete image and the experience they associated with it. "Hot Sun," "Sioux City, Iowa," and "On Monhegan Island" grew out of this assignment.

Autonomous Poems: These poems were gifts, born of the giftedness of the writer, out of the desire to make a gift to others, and the desire to give definite shape to what he had been given to work with. A few were gifts to me, and some, like "Words," were gifts to the writer—the poem suddenly present in the mind, and the poet, fully awake, and taking dictation from the inner stream of his own thought and feeling, let it come through, and was himself astonished at what he had given birth to.

These poems were entirely autonomous acts: "A Bad Dream," "A Pushkin Story," "The Poetry Group," "Marc," "G-d or Man," "Words," "Child's Lament," "Time Out of Control," "In Roumania," "Old Age Home," "Think of Others," "Withholding Judgment," "The Tuesday Poetry Group."

8

Songs of Healing

Shining Darkness

When I am asked what my sources are, and where I have found helpful guides for my work, I point to the medicine men, the poets and the *zaddikim* who, for all their large difference of custom, technique and rite, seem to be pointing to the same place—and it is a place intimately associated with old age and death.

The medicine men, the poets and the *zaddikim*—the makers of the healing songs of their tribes—have known since ancient times how to summon powers of healing which, like gods, "reside in the human breast." They have spoken the words which touch and contend with our darkness, and which revive our basic and regenerative trust: trust in the self, trust in the other, and trust in the life that flows through all sentient beings.

"The one Life within us and abroad" has been invoked by many names, in many places. It is the power we summon to us, in our need; and it is the power of the summoning itself. It is the real and ancient source of the poetry groups, and nowhere is it summoned more simply and more beautifully than in this Yuma medicine song:

Your heart is good.
Shining darkness will be here.
You think only of sad unpleasant things.
You are to think of goodness.
Lie down and sleep here.
Shining darkness will join us.
You think of this goodness in your dream.
Goodness will be given to you.
I will speak for it, and it will come to pass.
It will happen here.
I will ask for your good.
It will happen as I sit by you.
It will be done as I sit here in this place.

The Bushman Medicine Man

A friend of mine, Mel Konner, came to the Young Israel Club to talk about the Bushman, with whom he had lived for two years. He had studied their child-rearing practices, written poems about his life in their country, apprenticed himself to their medicine man, and taken pictures of everything.

He showed us a slide of the medicine man, recumbent, in a white blouse; his entranced head, heavy with his vision of heaven, was being tenderly held by a pair of hands that reached down from the top of the frame. And Mel told us where the medicine man had gone, and of the great contention which now engaged him, at a far remove from his body. He was arguing with a father in the spirit-world who was calling his young daughter back to him.

The medicine man was saying: "She will come to you eventually. You must wait. It is not right that you take her now."

But the father was alone in the spirit-world, and craved the companionship of his daughter. And the girl lay on the earth, unconscious, between life and death.

The medicine man was angry and persistent. He refused to give up the girl, and spent three hours arguing with her father. In the end, he persuaded him to be patient, and to let his daughter live out her natural life. And, knowing a father's grief, he gave him these words of consolation: "She will come to you in a while, but let her come in her own good time." The father reluctantly let go of his child, whose spirit returned to her body. Later that day, she sat up and asked for a drink. In a few days, she was well.

Before the medicine man came into his power, he had been sick unto death. His older brother, who had recently died, came down to the earth, bringing with him the wife he had taken in the spirit-world, to show that all was well with him, and that there was no cause for excessive grief. The brother and his wife sat in silence at the threshold of his hut, and watched over him. Then the wife walked a little way off, and the brother spoke: "Why are you lying there like that? I don't like it one bit. Get up and start moving around. Listen. Remember that song we used to sing together when we did the medicine dance? That is your song now. Get up and sing it. Teach it to the people. Sing it to them and touch them while you are singing it." Then the medicine man rose up and did the medicine dance. He touched the people, singing the song that was now his own, and which he henceforth sang when he did his medicine dance.

Mel Konner stopped speaking, and it was as if the whole room were holding its breath. Then several women burst out at once: "Do you know that song? Can you sing it for us?"

It is not strange that orthodox Jewish women believe in the miraculous power of a Bushman's song, believe in it enough to ask that it be sung for them. It is the song we all yearn for.

Poverty and Riches

I once read about an Eskimo woman who had never received her own song from the spirit-world. No greater poverty could befall a person; and she died without finding her song. For this, her husband wept greatly.

The medicine man, on one of his field trips to heaven, happened to meet the woman—and behold! she was singing. He rushed back to earth and told the grieving husband that he had seen his wife; and that, in dying, she had discovered her own song. She was now in the spirit-world, singing.

The man put off his mourning at once, and danced for joy.

Dream Education

Among the Senoi of Malaya, each person receives an intensive "dream education" that fosters an open and trusting relation to the life of the unconscious. Dreams, rather than being suppressed, are accorded a vital and honored place in their culture. At breakfast, each Senoi child tells his father and older brothers what he dreamed the previous night. He is encouraged to recapture the quickly-obliterated voices and images; and, gradually, he learns how to bring back great riches from "the other world."

In his dreams, he discovers poems, songs, medicines, dances, traps, truces, the gifts of peace and well-being, the resolution of conflicts, and the means of regaining mastery over uncopable realities.

Kilton Stewart, a research psychologist who spent a year among the Senoi, tells a story which exemplifies the "dream theory" of the Senoi. A young man found some gourd seeds and shared them with his friends. Everyone got diarrhea, and the young man was humiliated. That night the spirit of the gourd seeds came to him and made him vomit, showing him the purgative value of the seeds he had found. The gourd spirit also taught him a medicine song which he could teach his people. At the daily gathering, where all the men of the tribe came to exchange and discuss their dreams, the young man made a contribution which both benefited his culture and restored his self-esteem.

Senoi "dream education," like the dreamwork seminars of Fritz Perls, enables a person to grow by teaching him to integrate the "opposing forces" which he carries within himself. When a Senoi child has a falling dream, his father tells him: "That's a wonderful dream, one of the best dreams a man can have. Where did you fall to, and what did you discover?" The child, naturally frightened, answers that he broke his fall and woke up. "That was a mistake. The falling spirits love you. They are attracting you to their land, and you have but to relax and remain asleep in order to come to grips with them. When you think you are dying in a dream, you are only receiving the power of the other world, your own spiritual power which has been turned against you, and which now wishes to become one with you if you will accept it."

The Power to Cure or Curse

The Tuesday Group read, with considerable interest, the following words of Don Juan, a Yaqui *brujo*, or sorcerer:

"Ask yourself, and yourself alone, one question. It is a question that only a very old man asks. My benefactor told me about it once, and my blood was too vigorous for me to understand it. Now I do understand it. I will tell you what it is: Does this path have a heart? All paths are the same: they lead nowhere. They are paths going through the bush, or into the bush. In my own life I could say that I have traversed long, long paths, but I am not anywhere. My benefactor's question has meaning now. Does this path have a heart? If it does, the path is good; if it doesn't, it is of no use. Both paths lead nowhere; but one has a heart, the other doesn't. One makes for a joyful journey; as long as you follow it, you are one with it. The other will make you curse your life."*

In this teaching, the group keenly felt the presence of old age and death, not as enemies of life, but as bringers of clarity and freedom. Don Juan was affirming that only in the full consciousness of his mortality, in the knowledge that all paths lead "nowhere," could a person abandon his acquired notions of higher and lower, and freely choose the path that would allow him to live according to the dictates of his heart. The text asserted that a person's well-being was connected with his ability to make wise decisions for himself, and the key-idea touched off the following poem:

Decisions

I decided not to take the bookkeeping job on the spur
of the moment because it didn't leave me enough leisure
time.

I decided to retire because I was tired of getting up
at five in the morning.

When I come to do it, I do it by intuition.
When I come to the bridge, that's when I decide
how to cross it.

I decided to quit my job because there was too much
pressure and I thought I'd get along better without it.

I decided to take my oral English when I was told
that there were terrible pressures, there were eight
people who would examine you, and they would ask you
to talk on things you knew nothing about—like medical terms.

* Carlos Castaneda, *The Teachings of Don Juan* (New York, Ballantine Books, 1968), pp. 105-106.

I put my head high up in the air and I walked in
and I passed.

A friend and myself decided to go on a vacation,
and everything I suggested she found fault with, and
then and there I decided to go by myself.

I decided to get involved every moment I possibly
can, and I find it a great challenge.

I decided not to work with the aged and the infirm in
the nursing home because I felt I would be happier and
of more value in other types of volunteer work.

I decided to stay single and not marry again because I
value my freedom higher than my responsibility to a man—
and to be able to make my own life, to be able to give
of myself and have time of my own.
I made that decision twelve years ago and I'm not
sorry.

I can't come to any complete decision now due to ill
health.
My children urged me to take a vacation, and my wife
said: "Don't make reservations, you might have to break it."

I decided many things that never came to fruition.
Other people had control of circumstances, and I
wasn't a fighter.
I did want to go on a vacation, and my husband had
heart trouble.
Everything I asked him—I never got a yes answer.

Invalids can be tyrannical, they foist their will on you.
There was a time in my life when everybody was
trying to take over my thinking.
So I packed a valise and disappeared for a week.

I've never made a quick decision in my life.
There is always fear in a person, and it's so great
it monopolizes heart and brains.

I had a big decision to make.
This is my second marriage, 36 years we've been
married.
My first marriage was unsuccessful, I didn't
expect to marry again, for 3 years he pursued me and
wanted me.

I had a father who was a philosopher, we could
discuss everything, even sex.
   I asked him what he thought, maybe I was being narrowminded.
My father said: "He's a fine intelligent fellow."
He brought up my children and they love him.

   I was told this:
I was making a trip to Israel, I was having fears
of getting sick over there, and I discussed this with
my sister.
   She said, "Always you are going back and forth."
She brought out that I'm indecisive.

   I wanted to move, I didn't want to move, I had to move.
   I went to look at an apartment, I did everyone a
favor. I didn't want to take it, and then I was relieved.
   The fear of moving was terrible and when I finally
made the decision—thank God!

—Ann Rosenthal, Bella Jacobskind, Herman Balin, Leah Cahn, Libby
   Schindlinger, Rose Kitzinger, Sol Ehrlich, Dora Brown, Rebecca
   Feingold, Lilly Palace, Helen Palmer, Ann Branfield.

The Elm

   Keats said that if poetry does not come as naturally as the
leaf to the tree then it had better not come at all. And Rilke, in his
Letters to a Young Poet, also compares the artist to a tree: "Being
an artist means, not reckoning and counting, but ripening like the
tree which does not force its sap but stands confident in the storms
of spring without the fear that after them no summer may come."
Both poets, in the image of the tree, are speaking of the non-
volitional, or unconscious, character of creation, and of the health
and vitality of the poet. If the poet has a certain self-possession
and calmness of judgment during his own and others' crises, it is
because he finds them natural, like labor pains and rain in April.
And also, as in Sylvia Plath's "Elm," he never forgets or denies
what he once has known:

I know the bottom, she says. I know it with my great tap root.

It is what you fear.
I do not fear it: I have been there.

The poet, so often maladjusted to the great world, and considered by it to be a figure of maladjustment, is precisely the one who, at great expense, has made a terrible act of faith: he believes in an internal process, in the growth within him, even more than in the conventions which govern our careers in society. More than others, he has put his faith in the creature's natural powers of growth and can empathize everywhere with growing things, and feel a special reverence towards ripening, because whatever goodness has come to him has come from accepting his own particular way of growth. As he stands and stares down "the road not taken," he asks himself: "Does this path have a heart?" And then he goes his own way, affirming growth in his life and in his poems—growth in all its phases, serenity and storm; and everywhere, both in "This Compost" and "Out of the Cradle Endlessly Rocking," he is celebrating growth. Even in despair, he loves it wholeheartedly: his love may be sick with longing, it is nonetheless an act of faith.

Simple & Loyal Community

In his *Letters*, Rilke tells the young poet: "Rejoice in your growth, in which you naturally can take no one with you; and be kind to those who remain behind, and be sure and calm before them and do not torment them with your doubts and do not frighten them with your confidence and joy, which they could not understand. Seek some sort of simple and loyal community with them, which need not necessarily change as you yourself become different and again different; love in them life in an unfamiliar form and be considerate of aging people, who fear that being-alone in which you trust."

It is the poet's advantage, and to the advantage of the culture in which he lives, that there be some "simple and loyal community" between them. The famous image of Walt Whitman nursing the wounded Union soldiers comes to mind; and then, too, there are the poets who in recent years have gone into prisons, mental hospitals, ghetto schools, drug programs, into the places where the poor, the sick, and the aged are confined, because they, being poets, had laid aside—as Yeats said it is the business of the poet to do—"pleasant patter," and sought "the brutality, the ill breeding, the barbarism of truth." They could approach the people they worked with, not as "inmates," "schizophrenics," "junkies," and "dropouts," stigmatized creatures and outcasts, but as persons worthy of respect. And though the truth of their lives was brutal and their words ill bred, the poet, valuing their truth and their words, often could reach the imprisoned core of their health.

The Difference

If asked about the difference between the poet and another kind of person, I would say: There is none. And I would say: The difference makes a very great difference. And when pressed to clarify this paradox, I would adduce, among a number of possible explanations, the tribute of one great poet to another. Eliot, in an essay on Yeats, quotes a poem called "The Spur":

> You think it horrible that lust and rage
> Should dance attendance upon my old age;
> They were not such a plague when I was young;
> What else have I to spur me into song?

and then comments: "These lines are very impressive and not very pleasant, and the sentiment has recently been criticised by an English critic whom I generally respect. But I think he misread them. I do not read them as a personal confession of a man who differed from other men, but of a man who was essentially the same as other men; the only difference is in the greater clarity, honesty, and vigor."

That is a way of putting it. My brother, in conversation, offered another. He was speaking of his dreams, which are unusually vivid in their symbolism, and which he remembers with unusual clarity. He seems to be a natural child of the Senoi: his dreams are, for him, an important part of his life, and of his writing. What he said was: "The sheet of ice covering my conscious from my unconscious life is thin, so I can walk on water and see what's going on underneath."

Healers have traditionally walked on water, and poets have proverbially skated on thin ice.

"Tactus Eruditus"

In an essay on William Carlos Williams, Kenneth Burke tells the following story: "Some years after Williams had retired from his practice as a physician, and ailments had begun to cripple him, we were walking slowly on a beach in Florida. A neighbor's dog decided to accompany us, but was limping. I leaned down, aimlessly hoping to help the dog (which became suddenly frightened, and nearly bit me.) Then Williams took the paw in his left hand (the right was now less agile) and started probing for the source of the trouble. It was a gesture at once expert and imaginative, something in which to have perfect confidence, as both the cur and I saw in a flash. Feeling between the toes lightly, quickly, and above all *surely*, he spotted a burr, and removed it without the slightest cringe on the dog's part—and the three of us were again on our way along the beach.

"I thought to myself (though not then clearly enough to say so: And here I've learned one more thing about Williams' doctrine of 'contact.' "

This experience, Burke goes on to say, helped him understand Williams' praise of "contact" in art because he suddenly saw the connection between Williams' doctrine of contact and the two words which occur on a line by themselves in an early poem called "This Is My Platform": what he had witnessed was the meaning of "tactus eruditus."

The Way to Tell a Story

Martin Buber tells a story that was told to him by a Hasidic rabbi. This rabbi had a lame grandfather, who had been one of the Baal Shem Tov's disciples. One day the grandfather was asked to tell a story about his teacher, and he told how the Baal Shem Tov used to dance when he prayed. To convey the Baal Shem Tov's physical gladness, to make the remembered joy perfectly visible, the grandfather tried to act it out, and he began hopping around, the way the Baal Shem Tov used to do. In that moment, he was cured of his lameness. "And that," said the rabbi, "is the way to tell a story."

The Flute

One of the most famous stories about the Baal Shem Tov concerns an event which took place on the night of Kol Nidrei. It seems that, after all the prayers had been said, there was still no release, no flowing-forth of forgiveness. The Baal Shem Tov stood at the altar, fervently praying, but it was of no use. The Gates of Paradise remained closed.

Now, in the congregation there was a dull-witted, unlettered boy who had never previously been to the synagogue. Because he had reached his thirteenth year, his father had been obliged to take him, but he had warned him that this was a holy and awesome day, and that he had better behave himself. The boy sat in silence, as the others prayed, and he fingered a small flute, which he used to play while tending his father's sheep and cattle, and with which he called them.

After a long time passed, the boy said, "Father, I have my flute with me, and I would like to sing with it."

His father rebuked him, and the boy gave up any thought of participating in the service. Then the impulse came over him again. "Father," he said, "I would like to play just one note on my flute." The father took the flute away from the boy; and, once again, the boy sat in silence while the rest of the congregation poured forth its prayers and hymns. Finally, the boy could not restrain himself any longer. He grabbed the flute out of his father's pocket, and blew a loud clear blast. Everyone was bewildered and frightened—except the Baal Shem Tov.

Later, he said that it was the blast from the boy's flute which had opened the Gates of Paradise.

Holy Sparks

The Baal Shem Tov taught that in all things there are holy sparks; and that when the shoemaker makes a pair of shoes in his full strength, he releases the holy sparks that are imprisoned in his tools and in the materials with which he works; and whenever a person acts with his whole being, he transforms and hallows the world. If a moment should come when everyone in the world were to do all that he does in his full strength; if the lovers were to make love without indifference, if the warrior were to come to grips with his real adversary, and if the boy were to give out a loud clear blast on his flute, then in that moment the earth would be paradise.

Paradise

The only paradise I believe in is the one which comes fitfully, when we take back our daily flutes and let out our own dark or bright particular song.

Part Two

The Sessions

The Tuesday Group

First Session: A Thing Is Going on with You
Even if You Don't Welcome It

The first session of the poetry group on Tuesday was like a gathering of persons who find themselves in possession of a thing they have been unconsciously preparing themselves to have and share, and so are neither bewildered nor elated.

The session had been prepared for in a variety of ways. Two of its members, Bella and Lilly Palace, having worked with me elsewhere, were no strangers to a poetry group.

Nor was I a stranger to anyone in the room. For the past two months, I had been organizing a Tuesday Club, and in a setting in which I was a familiar figure—JASA's District Office in Brooklyn. So today, when I announced that I would be holding a poetry group in my office, everyone approached the group after a considerable amount of contact with me as their social worker, and they came to the group willing to extend their good will because of my part in helping them set up their club.

Nor were they strangers to each other. For two months, they had been working together in club-creating activities. The poetry group was part of a human continuum which included preparing meals and eating lunch together, planning political action in behalf of senior citizens, organizing recreational activities, discussing budgets, setting up committees, dividing up the responsibility for running the club, and handling emotional emergencies.

The previous contact made for a situation in which introductions of all kinds could be dispensed with. It was possible to plunge right in. I simply threw out a line that Joe Chaikin had used to begin a chant in an Open Theatre improvisation, a line from one of the rabbis: Let there be peace, and let it begin with me. I said that we were going to make a poem together, that each one in the group would contribute a line, expressing the thing that he or she most deeply wished for, the state or condition of things that he or she would most like to bring about. I told them I would take down their words as they spoke them, but that they should be less concerned with "composing" a poem than with telling the truth. They seemed at once skeptical about the whole procedure and excited about trying what, at the very least, might be an enjoyable game. What came out reflects their initial attitude, their understandable restraint in committing their hearts to their tongues:

> Let there be peace, and let it begin with me.
> Let there be health for our children.
> Let us have faith in God and the things that
>   are going to come.
> Let me hear what we've written so far so I can
>   add a good line.
> Let us walk hand in hand and not let go.
> Let us have love for all mankind.
> People have reached the moon but they haven't
>   reached peace in their minds and hearts.
> —Ann, Bella, Dora, Herman, Libby, Sophie, Berti

Dora's ironic-critical line not only disrupted the neat parallelism of the poem, it violated the "good will towards men" tone and broke into the "best wishes for a happy New Year" sentiment with the jarring and unquestionable sound of truthful expression. Our "nice" poem fell abruptly silent; and not-so-nice but very real people, provoked by authenticity, reacted with excitement.

After the laughter died down, Sophie said, "Well, that was a surprise." I said that good lines of poetry, like well-marshalled flanks, take you by surprise. Libby, a restrained person with a great deal of presence, said Dora's line was beautiful and true; and Ann, in her vehement and half-jealous way, also praised it. (It was she who had been anxious to hear what the others had said, so that she could "add a good line.")

The group's praise left the floor with Dora, who began: "When I get up in the morning and I can see and walk and talk, I'm a very happy woman." This touched off "A Play for Voices." What follows is a transcript, nearly verbatim, of the scene that unfolded in the group:

A Thing Is Going On with You even If You Don't Welcome It: A Play for Voices

Dora:
When I get up in the morning, and I can see and hear and walk and talk, I'm a very happy woman.
That makes me look forward to come here and be young.
Otherwise I wouldn't come into this tumult.

Ann:
I keep myself occupied, and my friend says: Ann, when will you stop running?
I say: When I stop running, will you come and hold my hand?
When I stop running, God help me, I don't want to be around.

Libby:
We all voice that same thought and we are grateful.
And I want to ask people to be tolerant if we transgress a little.

Berti:
I want to ask this question: why do we do things?
When I'm all alone with what I do, I wonder: why do we do the things we do?

Bella:
We can't control it, we do it by impulse.

Berti:
What I do now, is it fate?
A thing is going on with you even if you don't welcome it.
Every morning I get up and ask: why?

Dora:
She lives alone and because she's by herself she can see her life.
When she's in the tumult, she forgets herself.
That's by every person the same.

119

Berti:

It's my conscience that bothers me all the time.

Dora:

Do you remember the question I asked you this morning: What do
    I need it for, why bother with all this tumult of people?
It's in my bones.

Berti:

Something is happening that I'm perturbed about. I can't get rid
    of it.

Dora:

You're too far gone, you can't stop.

Ann:

Maybe she's beyond peace, her mind doesn't relax.

Berti:

I'm not involved with it alone.
When I wake up, I tell myself: O.K., it's finished. I want it to be
    finished.
But it doesn't finish.
In two or three weeks, I'm looking for him again.

Dora:

In Russian we say: It's hard to drive out and it's hard to swallow.
Is this a Platonic love?

Berti:

I want to answer you with a question. If you don't care, how can
    you care?

Ann:

Love is stronger than the biggest police force.

Dora:

Besides we get used to things, take my landlady's hello. She's an
    ignorant woman, but she says hello, every morning.
One day she didn't say hello to me, I was lonesome for her.

Herman:

She is hard on decisions, it's very human.
It's nothing wrong, it's a mixed feeling.
I am the same, it takes me a long time to make up my mind.
It takes me a long time to make up my mind.
I talk it over with my wife, she convinces me the other way.
Stronger characters, one, two, three, they decide.

Libby:
I want to know: what is the attitude of the other party?

Berti:
Let's say he asks for French Fries.
I say: You had too much already.
He gets everything as far as food is concerned.
But a drop of a pin could break it off.

Dora:
I want to know: who calls who?

Berti:
I call him.

Dora:
Wait for him to call you, that's self-respect.
He knows you need him more than he needs you.
Don't be a *shmatta,** even for your children.
You can't buy no love, even your own children's.
If you need him more, he will treat you like a *shmatta.*

Sophie:
Today's women are liberated.
Let her call if she's ruled by her head and not her heart.
Don't make a *shmatta* out of her.

Dora:
You're sounding like Isadora Duncan.
Isadora Duncan was a dancer, an *aussgelossener.†*
She said: Why can't I go out and ask any man, pick up every man?
Just because she don't take any money, she's not a prostitute?

Ann:
Here's what I say: take the good, what you seek in him, and overlook
    the other part.
If it gives you not to be alone, take the good.

Berti:
He's a bachelor, he's used to being alone.
I never lived alone, I can't stand it.
He's almost not human.

* *shmatta:* rag.
† *aussgelossener:* a loose one.

121

Ann:

Some are givers, others are takers.
Some are bigger givers, others are smaller takers.
Especially bachelors.

Berti (to Marc):

If you'll be a bachelor, I'll hate you.
A bachelor should be hated.

Herman:

A bachelor is not normal.
He's like a vegetable.
He's not broken in with himself.
If he has no real feeling for you, let it be finished.
If you are content with the good things, then stay with him.
You are an intelligent woman.

Berti (pointing to her head):

Nobody home.

Herman:

Nobody can advise you.

Sophie:

I worked as an accountant, I always make a balance sheet, I add
   up the good and the bad.
If you get more good than bad, then stay with it.

Dora:

You are not a sick person.
A doctor has to come to the sick ones, but you came to us.
I got the greatest respect for you because you expressed what's in
your heart.

Libby:

It's time to stop torturing yourself.
Let things take their course.
Whatever has to happen will come normally.
You come with nothing and you go with nothing.
Wake up in peace.

This is at once a completely unfolded playlet, and a working-
through of Berti's indecision—an indecision by which she feels torn
apart. It was revealing and saddening to watch her hands: as she
spoke, they fluttered nervously, continually picking at each other,
first the right, then the left, her inner battle in miniature.

The group allowed for and drew out her story, respecting the limits she wished to preserve. Dora was the most direct: "Is this a Platonic Love?" Everyone laughed at this, and at the mocking tone in which she rebuked Sophie's woman's lib line: "Just because Isadora Duncan doesn't take money, this doesn't make her a prostitute?"

Dora is an exciting person to have in the group, a real provoker, but also she can be dreadfully harsh. What is not in the transcript are the moments when I intervened, and I intervened to protect Berti against Dora's harshness. Dora is funny, smart, on target, and sometimes cruel. For example, she told Berti at various points that she lacked stability, had a weak character, was sick; not responses particularly conducive to helping Berti—who already is so self-tortured—find a way out of her dilemma.* The thing she needs, since she is so little able to forgive or accept herself, is not a harsh judge, but simple acceptance; tolerance by the group of her indecision so that she may learn, if not to resolve the issue soon or in the near future, at least to accept that she can feel two ways about a man, and that strongly.

Libby's words in the end were apt and lovely. They came after my unrecorded words to Berti, asking her to be a little more patient with herself; and since it was clear she was not yet ready to decide whether to leave him or to stay with him, I asked her to give herself time to make a decision that she would be sure would be right.

I felt the group was productive and helpful for Berti. However, much to my regret, she did not return next week, and when I went out of my way to invite her the following week, she said she had to rush off after lunch. Clearly, the group disturbed her. I had hoped that Dora's about-face, saying, in the end, that she had great admiration for Berti's openness and trust, along with the support she had received from the others, would encourage her.

It is also clear what low self-esteem she has. When Herman said he felt confident she could make the right decision, being an intelligent woman, she pointed to her head and said, "Nobody home."

* I regretted suppressing the exchanges between Dora and myself, but I was guided by my concern for Berti in preparing the text for the group's use in the following session.

Second Session: The Road Not Taken

At the second meeting of the group, I wanted the group members to examine something that was, for the members, recognizably a poem, that is, something that came equipped with all the outer trappings of what, for people who have not yet made its acquaintance, makes a poem, and also a poem that would have direct bearing on what had happened in the last session. I remembered an impressive article in Leedy's book,* a rather striking example of how a particular poem broke through to a woman whose anguish, like Berti's, was connected with her indecision as to whether or not to leave a man. The poem was Frost's "The Road Not Taken"; and the thing that got through to her was that the poet made and affirmed a difficult choice in full awareness of what he had given up.

The Road Not Taken

Two roads diverged in a yellow wood,
And sorry I could not travel both
And be one traveler, long I stood
And looked down one as far as I could
To where it bent in the undergrowth;

Then took the other; as just as fair,
And having perhaps the better claim,
Because it was grassy and wanted wear;
Though as for that the passing there
Had worn them really about the same,

And both that morning equally lay
In leaves no step had trodden black.
Oh, I kept the first for another day!
Yet knowing how way leads on to way,
I doubted if I should ever come back.

I shall be telling this with a sigh
Somewhere ages and ages hence:
Two roads diverged in a wood, and I—
I took the one less traveled by,
And that has made all the difference.

---

* Dr. Robert F. Jones, "Treatment of a Psychotic Patient by Poetry Therapy," *Poetry Therapy*, ed. J. J. Leedy, M.D. (Philadelphia, J. B. Lippincott, 1969), pp. 19-27.

Berti was, unfortunately, not there, and so the poem could not be used to carry forward the discussion begun last week. My stress, in presenting this first poem, was on what the Jesuits in meditation call "composition of place": clear visualization, so that, in its most immediate aspect, the poem would not be opaque.

My aim, then, was that they "get" the poem, because many group members, in particular Ann, spoke of the difficulty and unfamiliarity of poetry; and where, for example, Lilly Palace and Libby were excited in discovering what and how the poem meant, Ann reacted anxiously to the challenge the poem presented. She kept referring to herself and the group members as "laymen" for whom it was difficult to see the things I was pointing to.

Libby was quick to grasp that the speaker was about to go on an "unchartered way"; and, when I asked why he spent a long time looking down one road, and then, with apparent abruptness and lack of similar precaution, took the other, Libby said, "He's wondering what he's missing," and she realized that the speaker was in a state that Perls calls "creative pre-commitment"; he had, beforehand, inwardly settled on his choice, but before he could go through with it, he had to stand there, at the crossroads, investigating the other side.

Dora reacted strongly to the element of loss in the poem. "Whatever we do, we regret." But Lilly challenged this view, saying the speaker had obviously made the good choice for himself.

The main focus of concentration, however, was on "visualizing the meaning." I felt that leaving the room with a vivid picture in their minds would be a lot, for their first encounter with a poem.

We looked at the poem after reading the work of the previous week. A rather heated discussion developed about bachelorhood. Lilly Palace, not present when the "Play for Voices" was made, attacked Herman's statement that a bachelor is almost not normal; Herman, by the way, was not present in this session, and Bella demanded to read his part.

Bella spoke about her father, a widower, married only four years when his wife died; and, hearing Lilly, she objected to Herman's statements, although she had not said anything the week before.

Then Dora, in her forceful way, spoke up. "In the Sanhedrin,*

* Sanhedrin: the council of 72 elders in ancient Israel.

125

they didn't take unmarried men. They are not normal in a way, people are looking at them with *such* an eye." An evil eye, presumably.

While Dora was speaking, Bella, unusually silent the week before, feeling somewhat crowded out by all the new members in "her" group, kept repeating, "Oy, oy, oy." She feels particularly challenged by Dora, who is as expressive and emotive as she is, and as firm in her opinions. So the clash between the two women touched the surface: Dora, opposing bachelorhood and citing Biblical juridical precedent; Bella, supporting it, appealing to the facts of her personal life.

When I asked Bella, "What does the 'oy, oy' mean?" she merely shook her head, in quiet resignation, as if to say: "It's not worth arguing with *that* woman, but she couldn't be more wrongheaded."

Libby, the voice of reason, intervened. "We feel this way about single men as an outcome of our pattern of society. They didn't continue the generations so there is little sympathy for them, and they didn't culminate this pleasure in our existence, they're losing something." Libby went on to say she felt sorry for them. Dora stridently added that they lacked intelligence.

Libby, in a wonderfully pert retort, said, "Well, you know, they could always have a woman on the side."

Dora: "On which side?"

Dora insisted there was a great difference between marital sex and sex between unmarried partners; there was "no continuance."

Bella, unable to remain silent any longer, said archly: "What about Molly Picon, she adopted a child."

Now it was Dora's turn to shake her head in a resigned way, indicating that it was hopeless to argue against such a senseless opinion.

Someone, I think Lilly Palace, who is Bella's close friend, asked that we change the subject and do the Frost poem.

The dominant reaction of the group, experienced by Rebecca, a new member, Lilly Palace, and Libby, was their pleasure in having worked out the poem, and their sense that they were "learning again" and "keeping their minds active."

At one point, Ann and Libby started to take notes, which I discouraged. I said that it was more worthwhile to give their concentration to the discussion at hand, and to have enough confidence in their memories to believe that what was important for them would stay with them. Since fear of losing their memories is quite prevalent among them, I stressed that in the group they would learn that, if they involved themselves in the moment at hand, it would leave its impression, and they would learn that they could trust their memories.

Third Session: Lifting Illegal Nets by Flashlight

Here, again, the focus was on the poem: one of James Wright's wonderful poems about loneliness, sharply visualized, yet non-discursive, unlike Frost, enigmatic, with the poem culminating in what for Williams is the moment of contact: when we brush against something hard to name, some "old phosphoresence of life," and we are dazzled.

Lifting Illegal Nets by Flashlight

The carp are secrets
Of the creation: I do not
Know if they are lonely.
The poachers drift with an almost frightening
Care under the bridge.
Water is a luminous
Mirror of swallows' nests. The stars
Have gone down.
What does my anguish
Matter? Something
The color
Of a puma has plunged through this net, and is gone.
This is the firmest
Net I ever saw, and yet something
Is gone lonely
Into the headwaters of the Minnesota.

It's a dazzling poem, spoken in what seems a flat voice, in common speech, and I was interested in presenting a contemporary, and meeting head-on any resistance they might have to this as poetry.

There was none. There was curiosity, bewilderment, misunderstanding. Ann. once again, felt discomfort about not knowing it all right off, and launched into her spiel about how it was O.K. for me to be able to understand it because I was a professional, but they were just laymen. My response was brief and firm; it was mainly aimed at reassuring her.

When both Bella and Dora cut loose and came out with two lovely "spontaneous utterance poems"—Bella spoke about what she had seen "Under the Sea," and Dora spoke of "The Mermaid"—Ann continually interrupted them by way of a too-too persistent agreement. I asked her to be a little more patient and attentive in listening and said that she had broken the flow of both women's speaking.

Robin Shamitz, a vocational rehabilitation counsellor, was sitting in on the group, and later commented that Ann's manner had struck her, reminding her of someone who finishes sentences for you because he really can't stand to hear what you are saying.

One thing that occurred to me during the group was to ask each one to pick out the two words in the poem that for them were the most meaningful. Their choices were:

Dora: nets and luminous.

Rebecca: anguish and lonely.

Robin: anguish and net.

Libby: frightening and anguish.

Ann: flashlight and "plunged through the net."

Bella offered an entire line—"The poachers drift with an almost frightening care"—and so did Herman Balin: "Something/ The color of a puma has plunged through this net, and is gone." Herman's is the line of dazzlement.

We discussed as many of the word choices as we had time for, noting most had picked feeling-words, and the most oft-repeated object-word in the poem. There was some discussion of the patterned language of the poem: dark words, light words, and so on. But the main thing was the surprising relation which the speaker develops with the carp that he questions, and to which he extends, in the end, his empathy.

Fourth Session: Hostile Territory

Today, while conducting the other business of the club, I am bombarded with questions, complaints, anxieties, and the general chaos that precedes an outing; it is six weeks away, and the old

128

women come up to me in a steady stream all day, mindless of everything else that's going on, and ask: "Can I sit next to Sadie?" "Yes."
"Why can't I go on the bus, we're angry with you." "Be angry."
"Is that all you can say?" "If I could take you by helicopter, I
would." "It's not right!" Hammering, hammering: only rarely do I
lose my patience. Today I am firm and when the same woman
pesters me for the fourth time, angrily, bitchily, as I am working
out next week's menu and ordering food, I tell her off. She leaves,
tears in her eyes; her older sister comes and lectures me: that I must
not be petulant and it is unjust that they don't have seats on the
bus. Regathering my self-possession, knowing I have allowed myself
the luxury of one self-protective explosion, I explain everything, for
the millionth time, calmly, calmly, calmly—that it was sad they were
absent when the bus tickets were being sold, that the bus holds 45,
that I would be happy to take them on the bus, if I could, but I
can't. As Ken Kesey says: "You're either on the bus or off the bus."
They're off the bus, off the bus, and they've been off the bus all
their lives. For this, I am, occasionally, the target of a lifetime's
accumulations of petty grievance; and the recipient, when I provide the bus, of the gratitude of the old people which is something
like the gratitude of orphans, beggars, and cripples.

With everyone cramming me about the bus, and everyone else
cramming Mrs. Rachman, today's speaker, to sign up for a guided
tour of the Jewish Metropolitan Geriatric Hospital, I have two
thoughts now in my mind:

Speak to Berti before she gets away.

Get the poetry group going because it's already twenty minutes
late, the members have been waiting—an eternity—and how long
will their patience hold? And: we simply don't have much time
left in the day.

I sit in my office, giving my attention to each speaker, knowing
that each one has waited a long time for his or her "audience." After
a day of being pulled at, it's no longer easy for me to receive even
the ones I like with the outgoingness and warmth I usually feel. I
think, as I am being complained at for the fifth week in a row that
the free lunch lacks this or that: "I cannot give her what she wants,
and it's O.K." I am reassuring myself. It's not easy to say no, I
listen, again patiently, speak mildly, and I'm being tugged at inside. How do I react to demands I cannot or will not fulfill? Not
easy for me: I inwardly feel pushed and defensive and I over-

explain why the request cannot be met. And yet I am also free of assuming unreal responsibilities, and simply listen to the request, and if it sounds like a good idea to me, but one which I can't take responsibility for, I tell the speaker, "Well, that sounds fine. How can you go about getting it?" If he or she shows willingness to take part of the burden—of getting a certain speaker, beautifying the room, or anything else that would simply mean a too-great over-extension of my energies, I help them go about it. But I make it clear: I'm not a sugar daddy, a cornucopia, a good provider of "satisfaction" in the Rolling Stones' sense of the word—mass producer and pacified clients.

I manage to find a few moments with Berti, alone in my office, and let her know I would like her to be in the poetry group.

She was not, it seems, altogether frightened off by her first session. She wants to come, she says, but her "friend" expects his dinner at 3 o'clock. She cooks dinner for him five days a week: he comes, eats and leaves. Again she complains that she can't stand to be alone. I ask her if it's possible for her to get a day off. She says she's been asking for one. She would like to stay later on Tuesdays, so she can be in the group, but he says: "You have every day free, and all the other mornings and afternoons to yourself." His answer is not strictly logical, but so far she has been kept in line by it, and by her fear of losing him.

I said she might feel less lonely if she had others to be friends with, not only the man she cooks for.

She said she had to go today, but she would speak with him again.

At the start of the poetry group I hand out the following text, from *The Way of Life:*

> Man at his best, like water,
> Serves as he goes along:
> Like water he seeks his own level,
> The common level of life,
> Loves living close to the earth,
> Living clear down in his heart,
> Loves kinship with his neighbors,
> The pick of words that tell the truth,
> The even tenor of a well-run state,

The fair profit of able dealing,
The right timing of useful deeds,
And for blocking no one's way
No one blames him.

We read Lao-tzu, and Herman begins: on the uses of water. "It carries messages, they throw bottles, and water brings it, for help. A man in life is there for a purpose, not only to eat, he has to fulfill his purpose." He sees the purpose-filling life as a running water.

Dora speaks up, to compare water and man. "Water and people are two strong elements, but water is the stronger element!" Dora's characteristic view: a struggle, a survival of the fittest, an overcoming of strong elements.

This remark moves the group towards what will become the poem. "It's a troubled world"; Libby tries to help her fellow man. Dora says, "The zoo is in the heart of man." Florence says of the life around her: "it is hostile territory." The last phrase, for me, is the way in. I ask: "What to do to make it good for yourself in a hostile territory?"

Herman begins speaking the poem: what is hostile for him is the change in the world, and the violence of the present world. Dora, quick, spicy, sharp, disagrees: violence and death belong to no age, they were always present in history. Florence, a newcomer who has not opened up much but who has followed everything intently, reveals her "pet peeve": now that she's more open, she's angry when she's not received.

And suddenly I *hear* Libby's continual pleas for tolerance and understanding: behind it, there's stands a great hurt, her sense of herself as acting kindly and not being treated with kindness in return.

Dora, who began the poem, ends it: "If I see them trying to step on me, I am trying to do the stepping." The group laughs, it is a laugh of release and admiration.

Hostile Territory

For me the hostile since I been in this country is how it's changed.
Now I see every day a change in life, I watch TV and I see wars
and muggings and holdups.
It turns out I had no incident but I feel it myself.

I live in a different world.

The fire engines ran on horses and the trolleys, but ever since I came here when it was the destiny of someone to get killed, they got killed just the same.

Theft has been all over since the world was existing.

I still fight the elements and overcome it.

My pet peeve is this: when young, I wasn't out to express myself. Now when I relate an honest thing that happened,
and I'm not believed,
it makes me angry.

I like to make up my own mind and I like everyone to
agree with me.

When younger I did the best I could, I haven't been happy.

I read a letter in a paper, a woman wrote in and asked: "What is the purpose of life?" Sometimes I wonder.

The hard thing for me was lack of love.

The hardest thing for me was to have a deep belief in people and to find my trust was misplaced.

The hardest thing for me was the struggle with loneliness, the struggle to keep alive, the struggle to go on and try to help that life should have a meaning.

Very little my grandfather knew how much pain it would bring me to be helpful to old people.

Many times you get back with stones instead of bread.

I'm annoyed when I know I've been conscientious and done the right thing and I'm misunderstood and not appreciated and I feel hurt and want to get it all off my chest—and I say, "Never mind."

I cope with circumstances.

If I see them try to step on me, I am trying to do the stepping.

From small people I don't get insultment.

    —Herman, Dora Balin, Dora Brown, Leah, Florence, Bella, Rebecca, Libby

Fifth Session: The Mermaid

Today, once again, the group was conducted after an emotional maelstrom: fifteen new people came, the food service broke down, and there were fights on all sides. The old people can be violent and cruel. Sitting and listening to both sides of an argument, trying to help each one hear and receive the other, and to no avail—at moments, the anger in me is stirred, and if I too were to lose my head and start shouting, it would be a chaos.

Today's major fight started when Mr. Pincus, one of the waiters, was kept waiting at the counter; Sara Magid, one of the women on the Food Committee, accused him of giving some people two portions. He was enraged, demanded to be given three more plates of egg salad, for which new members were waiting. He was further incensed at what he felt to be the injustice of Sara's going into the kitchen, taking the trays herself, and serving "her people." Why couldn't he also go and take? Sara said: "You're just a waiter. You're not on the Food Committee. Only the women who prepare the food are allowed in the kitchen!"

Sara, also being a waitress, didn't have to wait to get her plates; Pincus thought it unjust.

It turned out that there was a simple cause for the fight: there was no more food. Rather than tell Pincus this—for it is unthinkable for Jewish mothers to admit to running out of food—she had started scolding. It also turned out she was anxious lest her own lunch "be sacrificed."

Pincus stormed into my office, aggrieved. When I realized what the situation was, the first thing I did was send out for more food.

It took twenty minutes to straighten out the conflict between the two of them—twenty minutes during which I was also being complimented for conducting wonderful meetings and accused of not moving fast enough to pick up a second-hand sewing machine someone wanted to donate to the club. Why hadn't I taken care of it on Saturday? I said even God rested on the seventh day. Wonderful to tell, Dora—for it was she who had found someone willing to donate the machine—after saying she was judge and jury and would have to condemn me, showed a little sign of clemency, and ended with: "Well, next time you'll do it when I tell you to."

By the time the poetry groups begin, I am often tired and drained. Today, there was a long difficult "town meeting," in which I said that it was only natural, with the coming-in of a large number of new members, that there be growing pains. New arrangements would be needed to make room for the newcomers; the ship built to hold 60 now had to be remodelled to feed and house 85. New committees to be formed, arguments, applause, good suggestions, a raffle in the middle, a new system of food service worked out, a continual call for co-operativeness lest the 80-odd voices fly off in chaos—the general strain of trying to work things out with a modicum of real democracy.

It is a relief to me, after trying to hold together the club, and arbitrating disputes among people hopelessly embittered with each other; after the general roar of the large group, to come into the poetry group and hear a concentrated—and often passionate—interchange of individual voices.

We read Dora's "Mermaid":

Maybe you saw Esther Williams
in this picture, years ago.
The girl, she was a cripple
and confined to a wheelchair.
She saw the fish swimming by
and she rolled off her chair
into the water.
There she became a mermaid.
Her father was a strict man
and when he came home
he asked the maid:
'Where is my daughter?'
'There she is
in the water, swimming!'
The father nearly collapsed.
And the daughter, she created
her own life
because she knew better
than her father
the strength within her,
and that was her cure.

The poem provokes a storm. The entire session is spent discussing it.

Rose Kitzinger, whose first session this is, says that the girl has performed a miracle, thanks to her determination.

Lilly Palace says, "She was so ruled by her father, and that is what crippled her. She fell into the water and that was freedom. When held strictly in rule, we are crippled, we need freedom."

Ann's relation to the poem, and to the group, is an anxious one: she fusses about whether the girl's fall into the water was an accident or determined, willed.

Rose says, "It was the rage to live!"

Ann corrects her: "Urge."

Rose: "No, rage to live. There's a difference. The will to live is one thing, but sometimes it's a rage, you have to fight for it."

Rose and Lilly, the two active voices thus far, each repeats her view of the poem. For Lilly, it is "getting free"; for Rose; "will power." Much later, I comment that both have gone straight to the pulse of the poem and put their finger on the lines that throb with "interpretation"; the lines in the last stanza where Dora says the girl knew better than her father the strength within her, and that was her cure.

Libby now speaks up. She opens a new line of discussion, "The poem is just a fantasy."

Rose: It's a miracle!

Marc: Picasso once said art is a lie that tells the truth.

The question as to whether the poem can be dismissed because mermaids don't exist is put aside for a moment. Bella returns to what is the other central issue of the discussion: the identity of the father in the poem, and his relation to his daughter.

Bella: You can't blame the father, he shivered her,* he overprotected her, he was a good father. It's the same as in my life. My father when I was going to go to Israel was afraid and he said, "Did I raise a daughter to go labour in Palestine?"

"No," Dora says, "he was not a good father." Dora reminds Bella that Ben-Gurion's father, a truly good father, told his son: "Go to Israel and work."

This could be explosive, Dora and Bella are both intensely feeling women, and often came into conflict. Bella refuses to reply. And yet, happily enough, she doesn't sit and stew either.

Lilly: Overprotectiveness ruins a child.

Libby: But it's not true, it's a fantasy, a myth.

Libby cannot get past what is for her a complete barrier: the mermaid.

---

*shivered her: an unconscious Empsonian ambiguity or spontaneous quasi-Joycean pun which combines English shivering and Jewish mourning. He "shivered over" her, worried about her, felt an intense and trembling concern in her well-being. He also "sat shiva" for her, mourned her illness as he would sit down on the ground in ritual mourning for a member of his family who had died. He was simultaneously concerned and bereaved.

"O.K.," I say, "the mermaid is 'a symbol.' What does it mean to speak about the mermaid here?"

Lilly Palace: I once went to the museum and saw a picture of green horses, it's like poetry, fantasies that in return are realities.

Ann is still fussing. "Why didn't she do it before?" I wonder: what kind of explanation is Ann looking for? What do her questions mean? She is asking why the girl didn't leave her wheelchair before this. Why this question?

Dora's answer is fine. "It's not an impulse, she didn't have the guts before, that dream in her was there a long time before it accumulated the strength to risk."

Rose: The mermaid is her strength.

Florence: The mermaid is her freedom.

Rebecca: It gives life the energy to do.

Lilly Palace again and even more vehemently states her view: the girl is a captive, under the domination of her father, and now she has escaped.—How true is this of herself?

Dora: No, she's not a captive, she wasn't ripe enough before. These things are growing gradually.

I say that, like Dora, I see the poem as a poem about growth.

Ann: Why does she make up her mind when she sees the fish?

Dora: She's in her teens, she's going to be mature soon, but not yet. In her mind, she compares. If the fish can, I can.

Lilly: That is the culmination—when she rolls off the wheelchair.

I ask what does it mean to grow from cripple to mermaid, to make such a change?

Dora says the mermaid is the mature person, the completed person.

Herman, who has been silent, now drops a bomb. "A mermaid is impossible, it's just Hollywood trash, because Esther Williams swims good, to show her off, it's all *bubba meises*" (a Yiddish expression for which the equivalent is "a fish story" which, in fact, this is).*

---

* *"Bubba meise"* literally means "grandmother story" and has the same associations in modern Yiddish as "old wives' tale" does in English. The phrase, however, has an interesting history, and does not derive from the association of old women, garrulousness and improbability. The origin of "bubba meise" is itself something of a "bubba meise," or rather a "bovo meise." It began as a medieval romance in English

136

Dora: You're a pessimist. You are like the doctor who touches the pulse and his head is in the clouds so he pronounces the patient dead.

Herman: You're too much of a poetess.

He means this, in part, as an insult—but there is also a grudging respect for her. Everyone had burst out laughing at Dora's retort.

Florence (to Herman): You lack imagination.

Herman is a painter of still-lifes and landscapes, an artist, and is offended by this. Often, he has good things to say about poems and life, if he manages to reach across the barriers which certain dogmatically held religious opinions make for him.

Herman (not replying to Florence): She shouldn't get credit for this, she didn't make it up.

This raises an interesting question. Since Dora's "Mermaid" came as a response to Wright's carp, was spontaneous utterance, a recollection, and not even of first-hand experience, but of a film, in what way is this a poem by Dora?

I mention that Shakespeare, from whom dramatic utterance seemed to flow "as the tree puts forth leaves," didn't make up the stories on which most of his plays are based. What also comes to mind, although I do not say it, is Beckett's acerbic discourse in *Proust:* there he claims that "involuntary memory" is not only the source of Proust's masterwork, but it is also the great principle of selection by which the artist rids himself of mere journal-

---

called *Bevys of Hampton,* which was translated into Italian and called *Buovo d'Antono,* which was adapted into Yiddish and called *Bovo Bukh,* which went through a hundred different editions and was so much a part of Jewish life that when anyone told an unlikely story it was labelled "a bovo meise," and since Bovo—that medieval Yiddish knight—sounded so much like "bubba," and since the Bovo stories were meant as harmless amusement for pious women—they being debarred by their sex from the knowledge of Hebrew and all sacred and serious study—and since generation after generations of "bubbas" told and retold the Bovo stories, the old tale of the wandering knight became an old wives' tale.

And is it, perhaps, of more than linguistic significance that, in a culture so utterly dominated by males, a phrase connecting irrationality and magical powers should undergo a change of gender and end up in the feminine?

ism and recovers the elements and emblems of daily life that are the timeless "spots of time."

Lilly Palace takes up Herman's challenge. She was there, in the third session, when Dora "made" her poem; and she emphatically ascribes the poem to Dora's authorship: "It's *Dora*, this poem *is* Dora." Her response epitomizes what is one of the primary purposes of the group: to find the poem in the person, and the person in the poem.

The poem, as Lilly says, is Dora. It is "in character—her voice, her diction and vision. It is also, as we have discussed earlier in the group, a beautifully organized and complete thing.

Bella is by now itching to read her poem, "Under the Sea."

In a glass bottom boat in Israel
I saw such wonders under the sea.
I all the time thought
coral comes red like the necklaces.
Underneath they grow white like lilies.

We saw fish swim by.
There was so much electricity there.
Some fish were like triangles,
and they came in lines of black and silver.
The whole beauty is the way the fish
swim around the coral bushes,
the combination of all the colors
of the fish swimming around the corals.

It is a new world down under the sea,
and now I see this more than ever.

After her reading, she goes on with a stream of reminiscence about her visit to Israel. We learn that she and her husband had planned to go, but he died, and she resolved to carry out alone what they had planned to do together.

Ann, in her immediate response to Bella's poem, says, "You're inspired."

Rose, quick to become engaged, trades a few travel anecdotes with Bella: she also saw King Solomon's mines. Speaking of the death of Bella's husband, which cut off their longed-for journey, Rose says: "*Man tracht und Gott lacht*" (Man plans and God laughs).

Bella ends the session happily. She has had her chance to do her "aria," in speaking of "the dream of my life." She laughs gaily to me, afterwards. "Oh, Marc, who knew in my old age I would turn out a writer!"

Sixth Session: The Spontaneous Overflow of Powerful Emotion

I spoke briefly with Berti in the morning. She asked: "Can you pay me?" Pay her, that is, for her work on the Food Service Committee. No, I can't pay her. "If I got a paying job, I could give him the air—you know what I mean?" The "gentleman caller" she feeds, her bachelor, pays her $15 a week for his supper. "And he's too stingy to buy lunch, he's a stockbroker, but stingy, so he's hungry to eat at 4 o'clock."

She said she would try to come next week to the first part of the poetry group, but she would have to be home in time to feed "her bachelor."

In the morning, both Lilly Palace and Rose hand me poems they'd written during the week. I put aside the Blake poem I'd been planning to use—"The Angel"—have the new work xeroxed, and ready for use in the group.

This is the first time, in this group, that anyone has brought in poems written at home; and now today, two poems come in. Lilly Palace, once, at my suggestion, wrote a poem at home. But this one came unbidden, as did Rose's. My hunch is that it came as a result of spending an entire session discussing "The Mermaid."

I said it was a treat to have group members bring in poems; and, as far as I'm concerned, it means that the group, which for some is an oasis in the general aridness of their weeks, is irrigating their lives. It is like my refusal to allow Libby and Rose to take notes: I said they might trust their minds, their memories, to carry out what would be essential for them, and that it would come back to them when they would have use for it.

Lilly began the session by reading "A Bad Dream."

One night as I lay in my bed deep in slumber
I dreamt that I was at the seashore walking on the sand

All alone but happy
The waves rolled merrily along the shore
I watched & watched & wondered what the waves were saying
Time was forgotten as I viewed the great expanse of the ocean
Suddenly I realized darkness was upon me

As I turned to retrace my steps back home I became frightened
I was lost
I could not find my way back home
Tears rolled down my cheeks
My confusion & frustration was great
I kept repeating, "What shall I do? What shall I do?"
I suddenly felt a hand on my shoulder

My husband told me that I had had a bad dream
Later digging in my subconscious mind I understood that I felt
lost because my daughter was out of the country
I felt lost without her
We were always so close to each other

Ann was quick to comment: "Your daughter comes first, you
can't live without her, you want to be worrying about her, and so
you had this dream."

Lilly objected: this too much explained away the process she
was recapturing in the poem. "No, no, it was all unconscious, I
didn't know. It's like when I am at the seashore and I see the waves
coming in and I think: What's under the water? What are the
waves saying? I'd love to go under the sea and get acquainted."
Then, as for the darkness: "It suddenly comes on you. It was like
when I was walking in the country with my husband, we were so
engrossed in what we were saying—I love nature—even worms are
beautiful—we were so engrossed, and suddenly everything went
dark, we didn't even notice how the storm came up."

All the time she was talking, Ann was doing something that
she habitually does: agreeing vehemently in such a way as to
cut the other short. Violent "yes, of courses"; blows of "I understand" fatal to communication. Libby muttered something, and I
too felt annoyed.

I said to Ann that in her excitement and irritable reaching
after certainty, she was sometimes oblivious of the other persons
in the group, and that her onrushing line of questionings and her
sudden agreements often had the effect of cutting others short.

The group returned to discussing the poem, and Ann sulked.

"What's wrong, Ann? Are you feeling hurt?"

She said that everything she feels always shows on her face, she loves the group and has told all her friends about it, it means so much to her, she always tries to accentuate the positive, if someone is wearing a new blouse and she likes it she says so, she says it's a nice blouse but she doesn't say that the person has these and these faults.

"Yes," said Libby, "I noticed that. You're always throwing bouquets at people."

Ann said that she always has a good word for everyone, that people often don't take the trouble to find the good in others, and that it was unfair to cut her off when certain others in the group are allowed to go on and on.

I told Ann that I felt she was not alone in having difficulty in taking in what others were saying, and that she had brought up an issue that was fruitful for the group to be working with.

Ann's conflict with the others in the group had given rise to occasional mumblings, but had been for the most part suppressed. Now seemed like a good time to openly welcome it. I said that focusing on Ann's responses to others concerned everyone in the group, and that it was necessary for the development of a non-interfering free exchange among the group members. Only by hearing what we sounded like to others could we learn to hear ourselves more clearly, and only by learning to hear ourselves clearly could we develop the capacity to hear others. We were all, to varying degrees, hard of hearing, and the group could help us clean the wax out of our inner ears.

Since Ann was feeling rejected by me, I knew that she was having trouble hearing what I was saying, and that she viewed it solely as an attack upon her. So I asked the other members of the group what they felt I had said to Ann. I thought their response to her—their identification, acceptance and criticism—would help bring her back.

Libby said that almost everybody found criticism hard to take, but that it was important to know how to accept it. "We all have certain faults, and we're lucky if we have someone to talk to about them."

Bella said—and she was the one Ann had in mind when she spoke of the injustice of silencing some and letting others run on at the mouth—that I had told her to shut up, long ago, in the Thursday Group, and that she had learned something from it. She went on to talk about how the group had changed her: "When I came in, I was like a rock, now I can express my feelings, I came out of my shell, I'm all changed, it flows unconsciously out of me." I said that it had been painful for Bella, not only to come out of her shell, but to learn to give others a chance to come out of theirs, and Bella had had a rough time accepting it when I had asked her to listen and attend more carefully to what others were saying, and not charge in and overwhelm the conversation with her own out-flow.

Ann recovered her voice and said, "I have a moment of in-spiration, me you have to let to talk. Dora can be quiet, be quiet, be quiet. But I'm like Bella. With me—bloop! out it comes! I can't hold it back. I'm one of the ones who can't hold it back. If I don't get a chance—ooh! I forgot! It's gone, lost. We're all different. Some can accumulate, some can't hold on to it. Perhaps I should be one of the ones you let talk."

I was touched. I told her that I had never heard her speak so directly of her own needs, and that I found everything she said clear and right to the point.

I also said that it would be a good thing for her to learn how to hold it in, and all learning involved a letting go and a holding in, we had to learn how to let go and how to hold in, and we had to learn what to let go of and what to hold on to, and that this was the basic process of all growing. I said that by holding on, she would learn that she could trust her memory, she would learn that she need not fear losing her thought and her feeling, her moment would come round again, and then she would get a chance to speak, she would be as fully inspired as she had been before, when the exciting thought first struck her, but she would be letting it go at the moment when the situation was right for it to be received. She would find that the moment of her inspiration and the moment when other people were open to take her in need not be in con-flict. She could find ways of making them come together, and then, truly, what she had to say would not be lost.

Ann said, "It's not so easy to change at this stage of the game."

"It's not easy to change at any stage of the game. But if you want to, you can."

"Well, I keep coming back, don't I?"

"Yes," I said, "you certainly do."

The other event of importance today was Florence's revelation that she, too, had written a poem this week; that "my true self came out, but it was so morbid, I tore it up." Herman said to Florence that Pushkin wrote on morbid themes, on death, but—"what would be if he tore it up?" Something good had been lost. I was emphatic in picking up on what Florence said. Yes, she had been shocked by what flowed out, when she let her true self come out. But my feeling was: it was precious; it was, after all, her true self. And though with her conscious mind she might reject it, and see it as morbid, I was sure it was neither strange nor unfamiliar to anyone in the room, and that we'd all felt or thought the same at some time or another. Rebecca had felt depressed and that life had no purpose. And I, when my first true poems came out, felt naked and exposed; but they also happened to be the poems which a publisher was interested in putting before the world, as having some use. I also said: you might be surprised to find out how not-morbid the others would find it; that I wasn't asking her to show these things to anyone, but that if she wrote another such poem, not to destroy it, because a time would come, with mutual revelation creating more trust, when she would no longer want to hide such things.

After the group, I asked to speak with her alone. I told her how much I'd been touched by what she'd said. She then confided to me that the poem was about angry feelings towards her parents. I told her these feelings were normal and natural and everyone had them, at one time or another.

One of the members asked a question that vexes the beginning of every poetry group. She asked: "What makes a good poem?" A whole range of questions were included in this question, and she asked them: "Is this a poem?" referring to Lilly's poem. "What's the difference between prose and poetry?" She was, in short, asking for a definition of poetry. A question not to be ignored, or answered too quickly.

I said that by working with poems she would begin to form her own idea of what makes for good poetry. Since she was insistent on hearing something on the subject from me, I said a few words about saying a lot in a few words, spoke a bit about imagery, explained the difference between verse and poetry, and that a poem might even use certain forms. I said I would prefer to leave discussion of technical matters to their appropriate time, that is, in order to get at something particular in a particular poem.

The issue has come up in every group, cannot be side-stepped, but it is pointless to tackle it head-on. My answer is: let the poems do their work, and let working on poems take care of the answer. Every now and then, some "five minute non-lecture" on some aspect of poetry is in order, and I give it. I am not indifferent to their hunger for formal knowledge. But by and large, insofar as I teach this matter, I teach it by way of question and example.

Seventh Session: The Embrace

The antagonism, mostly covert in the past, between Dora and Bella, came to a head at the beginning of the group. Dora had brought in "A Pushkin Story," retold in her words, to refute Herman's charge that Pushkin was morbid. Bella had said last week she wanted to read something she'd written about the poetry group. Last week, for the first time since she's been in the group, Dora didn't say a word. Each woman wanted her due. Who would go first?

The moment each one made her claim, the other was incensed. Dora, in a huff, folded up her paper when Bella "dared" take out hers.

Lilly Palace: "I sense an antagonism. What difference does it make who goes first?"

Rose immediately asked me to decide, and I refused, saying I felt the group could handle the matter.

There was a silence, a deadlock, and several people spent time saying that the whole thing was a waste of time. Again, Rose asked me to step in; and again, I said I had confidence in the group to work it out, and that was what we were here to do.

Finally Lilly Palace announced: "O.K. Bella will be the big one."

I said I didn't think the question admitted of big and little, and gave my impression of what had been going on between the two women for quite a while: Bella, when Dora spoke, would communicate her indignation to Lilly by puffing up her face in a "There she goes again" expression; and, just in case Lilly didn't realize Dora was being offensive by merely talking, she would pull at Lilly's hem.

Lilly has a kind of maternal interest in Bella, and does not want to see her emotional protégé in any way suffocated or inhibited because she is all too sympathetic with "what Bella went through." Well, they've all gone through hell, and Bella does not have an option out on suffering.

I said that, quite often, when two highly expressive people come into the same room, there's a clash between them. I stated what I felt each woman's particular gift to the group is, and said that each has contributed enormously to the growth and vitality of the group. Simply by recognizing the fact of the two women's competitiveness and expressing the positive contribution of each, the matter was, superficially, settled. They each had gotten what they wanted: recognition.

Bella, with a better grace, yielded the floor—she was still indignant. Dora consented to read us her work.

A Pushkin Story

Writers are not pessimistically inclined, a writer writes according to his moods.

Pushkin was a very talented personality. One story I do remember of his, it made on me an enormous impression. The story goes as follows:

A rich landowner was given a ride by his servant, the carriage pulled by four pair of horses, fat and strong like the owner.

In front a poor farmer with a skinny horse could hardly move, the farmer belted the horse but without success.

The rich man said to the farmer, "Why are you belting that poor horse, he is so skinny and looks not well."

The farmer said, "My horse is lazy, so am I skinny and not well, but I work."

The rich man said, "Let my carriage go first, your horse will follow my horses unconsciously."

And so it happened.

What does this story represent? And what is your verdict to our beloved teacher and ladies and gentlemen?

With respect,
Dora

145

The little parable-like story left the group in a state of speculation, and a variety of interpretations were offered.

Libby: "The rich man couldn't make progress, he wanted the poor man to let his vehicle go first. There's some theory behind it. By the power of suggestion to the skinny animal he'll pick up speed."

The story is something of a Rorschach test, for Dora gave us a simple set of facts and left it up to the group to provide clusters of motive and meaning. Libby's interpretation was the most balanced and penetrating: she was aware of the rich man's wish for priority, but she also saw that the poor man derived some benefit; moreover, she provided a guess at the agency which moves the story: "the power of suggestion."

Lilly Palace was vehement in her reading of it. "It's about class distinction, the rich rule the poor and always get their way, this was Russia." As in her interpretation of the Mermaid poem, I remarked, Lilly focused on the conflict between the powerful and the powerless, those who dominate and those who struggle against domination.

The other Lillian in the group, a new member, had the reverse interpretation: the rich man was helping the poor man. The poor man was stuck on the road, beating his horse, and couldn't budge it. If he let the rich man's carriage go first, the skinny, abused horse would simply follow.

Florence: It's the herd instinct, people are like sheep.

Sol: It was a con game, a trick so the rich man could go first.

Interpretation, I suggested, was an act of creation: or, the poem is a co-joint act of creation between writer and reader.

Very well and good, but they wanted the definitive version.

Once again, an appeal to authority, me; once again, appeal declined.

Rebecca: Marc, ask Dora what it means.

Dora was sitting silently, patiently, enjoying the discussion her Pushkin story had evoked.

Bella, by the way, was grimacing and pulling at Lilly's hem throughout, and uttered not one word in the discussion of Dora's story.

Dora spoke: Psychologically, it's a case of monkey see, monkey do.

Dora loves to speak, and given the floor, she is often witty, biting, and hugely interesting. The group enjoys her as much as she enjoys to speak; and, in fact, has dubbed her "The Philosopher." Dora will, in general, not interrupt anyone; but, having patiently waited, she expects her turn; if anyone should venture a statement in the middle of one of Dora's Discourses, she will fix them with a rather fierce glance, and say, "You got your turn, no? Did I interrupt you?" The foolhardy one who ventured into speech while Dora was talking is silenced; Dora now reigns, and she gives us the story—loaded with epigrams and folk sayings—that she's been saving for us.

What Bella no doubt has difficulty with is Dora's ability to make herself heard, when she wants to be. Bella, of course, is equally capable of commanding the group's attention.

Dora now begins her satirical comments on mankind's frailties. "Psychologically, you often forget yourself. For example: if you devote yourself to pain, you got pain all the time." She then tells us a story about a woman whom she tended as a volunteer in an old age home. The woman was sick, but not all that sick, and couldn't sleep. She wanted a new pillow. There weren't any. Dora said, "I'll get you a new pillow." She removed the pillow, went to another room, puffed it up, brought it back, saying, "Here's a new pillow," and the woman fell asleep immediately.

In short, the rich man was helping the poor man.

Leah spoke up. She had worked on a farm in South Dakota; the cows ate thistles and she called, "Here, bossy, here, bossy." One cow wandered off, got stuck behind a barbed wire fence, and she left the herd to get her. When she brought back the herd, she was scolded: "You shouldn't have gone through the barbed wire to get that cow, she would have followed the others back."

Ah yes, the herd instinct.

Time to catch Bella, who is drifting away in hem-pulling feelings of anger and rejection.

Bella, in response to my question, "Where are you?" complains that this new group is not as good as the old one. "We got intimate, we trusted each other, we had confidence."

What's to keep her from getting intimate now?

"One wants to steal the show."

Who could that "one" be?

"I'm not naming names."

Rose: It's a clash of personalities. Let me read what I brought in, it may settle everything.

Request declined.

The two women have not yet said a word to each other. What's Dora's feeling about all this?

Dora: Bella treats me nice, when I come in she doesn't ask to see my card, she's like a mother.*

Unexpected goodwill. Dora got her turn, and now—she is genuinely friendly.

This calls for an adjustment of Bella's attitude; she hasn't been quite prepared for this. But here it is: Dora is feeling a certain amount of goodwill towards her.

Bella doesn't respond directly, but begins to become enthusiastic about the group. "We should be like a family, we're all lonely, we need friends. Thanks to the group, I talk out my feelings, I'm better."

She is beginning to relax and become the exuberant person who takes everyone to her great maternal bosom and whom the group quite genuinely likes for the feeling of lovingkindness she is capable of spreading around.

"Now maybe I can read this?"

Sure, why not.

Bella reads her piece.

I am in Marc's poetry group, and I want to express my appreciation what the poetry sessions gave me.

I am a widow, I live alone and most of the time I am with myself.

I was born in Warsaw, Poland and got a Jewish national education and with dignity and pride I carry my Jewishness, I am proud of our heritage and traditions that kept us alive as a people over 2000 years. I grew up in an anti-Semitic country where the life of a Jew is very hard and sad, and so are my stories I tell my group from my own life.

I am coming out of my shell, I can express my feelings, and I am happy that I can bring in a little Jewishness into my group.

We learned Walter Whitman's poem and also a beautiful psalm which I liked very much.

* Bella, as secretary of the club, sits at the door and, among her other duties, checks membership cards.

148

I have my inner satisfaction that I am able to bring
the Jewish spirit into my group.

The sessions with Marc are like a therapy for me and I am
thankful to him.

Bella's praise of the group and of me evokes applause; she gets
up and comes over to kiss me. We embrace.

Rose says this fits right in with what she brought, and she
reads "Marc," another piece written in gratitude to me.

> Poet, teacher and scholar, and yet he is much more
> He is a human being who cares about people and their feelings
> Though with much more education than most of us
> He sees all at eye level
> What greater attribute can G-d bestow on man?[*]
> After a session with Marc one feels stimulated
> You learn to listen and to really hear
> As for myself it always adds a little more joy and knowledge
>   to my day
> This is my way of saying, "Thank you, Marc.
> It's a delight and a wonderful experience
>   being in your group."

I am, of course, happy, but once again speak about how I
think the group really works—I think it needs to be insisted on,
when the members are about to overcredit me with the group's
success. I say that my satisfaction comes when I see the group members becoming more active and creative and overcoming difficulties
they have found impossible in the past; I remark, for example, that
I have noticed several small but important changes in the group
since we started; that the members of the group seem more willing
to pay attention, to listen, to each other.

In the conflicts of the past two sessions, Rose has stayed out of
the fray, even as she appealed to me for a chance to get heard.
Because she did not assert herself, she was pre-empted, and the
poem she brought in last week was not read. But now that Dora
and Bella have each gotten their hearing, and Rose herself has
poured on a heavy dose of the "let's kiss and make up" spirit, she

[*] G-d: Religious Jews do not write the name of God.

149

has her opening and takes it. She has gained more by wisely biding her time than she could ever have gained by challenging Dora or Bella. Now the group is entirely receptive to her. Having gotten the kind of attention she wants, having made a clearing for herself in the group, she reads her poem.

G-d or Man

It is difficult to write when one is sad
  and yet—I keep asking myself:
  was it G-d's will or man's blunder?
When a young lady goes for a check-up
  has a drug administered by the doctor
  and in five minutes a beautiful life is gone
  was this G-d's will or man's blunder?

When a young man has a doctor tell him
  he only has a virus
  and within one hour a wonderful life
  ceases to exist
  was this—G-d's will or man's blunder?

When young innocent lives are taken
  by wars, muggings and shootings—
  is this G-d's will or man's blunder?

Rose's poem evokes an urgent discussion of quite an old conundrum: How can there be death and evil in the world if God is good? What is the cause of the tragic deaths Rose speaks of? Dora is convinced it is man's blunder that has caused these things. Lilly Palace keeps repeating, "I want answers! What's the answer?" Dora: "That Congressman who was shot, he wasn't shot by heaven."

Rebecca has been silent all afternoon. "Where are you?"

Dora: Not here.

Rebecca: Depressed, it's so true.

She begins to cry, ever so slightly; her face is broken at the edge of tears, and tears well up in her eyes; she is on the brink of letting go of her pent-up sorrow.

The rest of the session is focused around Rebecca. Rose is particularly helpful and giving: "You should express yourself to others, I appreciate you, I'm occupied, but I understand your loneliness, sometimes it's so empty in my house. This group is made for people like us, we all have to talk here, but you—it's a must, you have to learn to talk."

Bella tells a long story about how she came through her "dilemma," the death of her husband.

Rose: Yes, and you have to force yourself to pick yourself up.

Leah: This helps me keep my sanity. A doctor once told me, "Someone in your situation they could put in a hospital, but you're lucky, write out your feelings, write and write it out." It's no lie, it saved my sanity. Poetry is a form of psychiatry. All the anger, you have to get it out.

Lilly Palace tells how she "forgot herself" and was helped, during a time when she was getting violent headaches, by painting pictures—pictures which are now on her living room wall.

Rose has a vault full of papers she wrote after her husband's death. "This was my outlet."

Rebecca has begun to smile; she says she will try to talk more in the group.

There follows a short active exchange between Rebecca and several group members—Rose, Lilly, Florence, Bella—in which Rebecca is encouraged. I tell Rebecca her homework is to get the phone numbers of two persons in the group and call them during the week.

More discussion of anxiety, depression, and loneliness overcome—through creative work and contact with others.

Dora (wryly): We're missing only one thing—the couch.

Marc: Don't worry, I already ordered it, it'll be here next week.

Several people suddenly come in to see me—urgent business. The group has gone way over—we must stop. The first thing that happens when everyone stands up, much to everyone's surprise, is that Dora runs up and takes Bella in her arms and gives her a long, long embrace. And Bella returns it.

Bella: Well, now it's a clean slate, we're friends.

Eighth Session: The Ingredients of Our Life

I began by asking Rebecca if she had spoken to any of the group members during the week.

Rebecca: The days are so short, and I'm used to being alone. People aren't interested, and I'm not interested in broadcasting, I'd rather listen, except once in a while, to give out a little bit.

Rose: Well, you brought us in Rebecca, we misunderstood you last week.

Rebecca: The news of bad—it made me lonely and depressed, it made it worse, but I didn't want sympathy.

Rose: Well, we were stupid enough to think you agreed with a great suggestion.

Leah: I was the one who asked if she wanted to take my phone number. I thought we could speak on the phone—not about problems, but something gay.

Ann: What do you mean, you don't have time?

Rebecca: Well, Marc suggested I take the phone numbers of two people, and I didn't say anything.

Rose: Why didn't you speak up at the time?

Rebecca: This group satisfies me temporarily.

Esther: If you have no time, it must mean you're satisfied with yourself, that you're doing something and there's no time to be depressed, that takes depression away.

Rebecca: I used to babysit, and then I was alone again, I lost a lot of sleep.

Bella: You're not alone, there are over twelve million widows in America.

Ann: Here we're all widows.

Dora: We are also short of time, she has momentary problems, by the moment we have to soothe her moods.

Ann: You should become active in the club.

Libby: She says her days are short, and she's occupied with something that sustains her, so where's the depression, so let's close it.

Rebecca: I have to snap out of it myself.

Rose was particularly disappointed with Rebecca for closing down after she had opened up the group. The truth is, as Rebecca made clear, that she had no intention of maintaining contact with group members during the week. It was, in fact, Rose who had really opened up, and in giving support to Rebecca last week, had revealed a side of herself she had never previously shown the group. Her anger, instead of being directed at Rebecca, came out when she said, "We were stupid enough to believe you wanted our help, and we were mistaken."

When the group was pushing her to become involved in more activities, I asked if it was O.K. for Rebecca to feel that coming to the poetry group was enough for her right now. Ann said, "Yes, it is, she might be getting enough here." I said that for someone so "used to being alone" I thought Rebecca was doing a lot for herself by coming regularly week after week and participating.

But to Rebecca I made another point. Her insistence on isolation, her refusal to accept sympathy, her feeling that she had to do it all by herself, warranted challenging. I did this by way of a parable, derived from the Pushkin story: an ox pulled a cart into a ditch on a wet day, and the farmer was stuck there, unable to move. Was it all right for him to accept a pull from somebody else?

Bella: "This pull I got from you, Marc."

Rebecca nodded.

Once again, several people brought in work to share with the group.

Rose told us about "New Windows on an Ancient Day: An Experimental Sabbath" which had moved her deeply. The prayers were in English, and the rabbi, during the service, had asked each person to turn to his neighbor and ask him how he was and if there was something he could do for him.

She read an article—or rather, a passage from an article—which said that increased emotional maturity is the goal of life, and the three cardinal virtues to grow towards are self-knowledge, self-control, and unselfishness.

Rose had begun making important contributions to the group: she has a keen grasp of what the group is all about; and, in her discussion of the passage, stressed that each member still had growth ahead of him, and more maturity to gain.

Dora read a piece on "independence for minorities"—she appears to be more aware of politics and political environment than the others. There was a polite non-response to this. Either they didn't take it in, or they did hear and wanted to avoid the rather controversial issue of Palestinian liberation. One doesn't usually think of old Jewish women espousing the cause of the Palestinians —another eye-opener. At any rate, nobody picked it up.

Leah read the poem she had written after the last session:

153

Words

Words are the gateway to the heart
Words are the windows of the soul
Words move mountains, words move armies
Do not betray their trust
Use them wisely, use them cautiously
Keep silent if you must.

The poem was received with a good deal of enthusiasm. In one of the exchanges it stimulated, Dora, Ann and Libby came out with the following:

The Boss of Words

You are the boss of your words.

Not always: you don't make any impression
  on a person who's not receiving.

As long as the words are in your mouth
  you are the boss.
The moment you let them out
  you are no boss.

Your words are changed,
  they are misinterpreted,
  you can no longer recognize them.

A word's not like a bird:
  a bird you can bring back.

In praising Leah's poem, Libby said she liked "the truth in it." What moved Ann was "the way it's said."

I introduced them, formally, to Metaphor—an old acquaintance of theirs, I told them, whom they had passed in the street hundreds of times, but now they were going to meet him and find out something about him by conversing with him.

Using Leah's poem as a starting point, they made "A Well-Mixed Cake." As they spoke their sentences about "words," I read back what they'd written, and paused occasionally to comment on a sentence in which something had been strikingly—metaphorically —put. By the end, they were less given to abstract statement and sententious and platitudinous lines and were speaking in full voice, making use of their familiar metaphors.

I think no poem has given the group greater pleasure, as a group, in the making. There was a sense of: "look, we're really doing it!" A line was added onto line, and the group got a sense of its abundance and fertility, the women became more and more like kids I'd worked with, laughing, clapping hands, congratulating each other—a general heightening of pleasure and responsiveness.

A Well-Mixed Cake

The words I heard about the young father's release
from a prison in Asia—I was relieved because he was relieved.

Words are a pathway of understanding, and words are
a road to dismay and sadness.

If we could build a coat of armor around our emotions,
words couldn't harm us.

Words brought happiness to this mother who heard her
son was still living.

When I need words the most, I'm at a loss for them.

Words are therapy, and the tongue is the main object
that makes it all clear.

A sharp tongue can do a lot of damage.

The tongue is the boss of the body. Life and death
depend on words—what the tongue speaks out.

Words are like a thunder—they can come down like a blast.
Words can be like a rainbow also—they have many colors.

Are words in the Bible the true thoughts of God?
Words of the prophets—they help us to live.

Words are the mountains of our imagination.
Words are the skeleton of our souls.
Words are the garment of our body.
Words are the heart of our everyday living.

Words have eyes to penetrate into the false and the truth.
Words are like a ripple in the ear—good news is
wonderful words.
Words have fears, and words have love and compassion.
Words have feet that lead us on.

Words have hands that soothe the sick.
Words have the secret source of a spring of water—
like the fountain of youth.

Words are the ingredients of our life.

> —Dora, Leah, Bella, Ann, Rose, Libby, Henrietta,
> Florence, Rebecca

Ninth Session: The Beginning and the End
The Word vs. the Slap

After reading last week's poem, "A Well-Mixed Cake," the group got into a heated discussion about which was more damaging: a word or a slap.

Yetta, a member of the original Thursday poetry group, returning now after several months, said: *"A pahtch fergayt, un a vort bashteht"* (A slap fades, and a word remains).

Florence: They are equally cruel.

Leah: It all depends on who it comes from.

Lilly Palace asserted that words were positively more hurtful, and vehemently defended this position against anyone who questioned or challenged it. When Florence reiterated that "any form of cruelty is cruel," Lilly argued her position with something of a religious fervor. "The sensitive individual will always feel the word more than the slap, I'm talking from experience."

Rose: People arguing can bring each other to tears, a smack will do less damage. The word is a sharp instrument.

Lilly: When my father spoke—he never slapped—I cried, it was like a deep wound.

Florence: That was *your* experience, mine was different. They are equally humiliating.

Libby: I'd agree with you, Florence. The poem is about adults. A slap is detrimental and insulting and leaves a lasting impression, but between children and parents it's normal.

This evoked, once again, vehemence of disagreement between Florence and Lilly, who struck me as a rather opinionated champion of open-mindedness.

Yetta: Well, it depends on different relations. My husband, if he hit me, it would be a blow, it would be terrible, but words can be crippling. I almost died because of what someone said to me.

As a general proposition or truth, the issue was not resolvable. I said that it was less important to decide, as a general rule, whether the slap or word was more hurtful than to accept the validity of each one's experience. Libby, more than any of the others, had the necessary detachment and sympathy to be able to do this. What was significant, I said, was that each one had been hurt, and deeply, and had said as much to the group, and that each one's general ideas derived from her particular experience.

Leah

Leah, whose poem "Words" had touched off the collaborative poem under discussion, asked me if writers were not continually discontent. I said that this was a popular belief, but untrue; that writers experienced both gratification and discontent in their work, like other kinds of workers; the gratification was as real and strong as the discontent—but more fleeting.

Leah said she had always been discontented with her writing. "It was a big step, to try to write again. I spent thirteen years writing, they said I was talented and that I should find a teacher. But this is the first I've written in years. Lillian inspired this when she said, 'Words are beautiful.' I thought to myself right off, 'Words move mountains, words move armies,' I thought of all the other things words do. You know, I was never really satisfied with anything. But last week I felt a way of going back, this group has done that."

"We inspire each other," said Lilly.

I asked her if she was content with her new poem, and she said that she was—but she seemed reluctant to say so.

Mr. Lerman

One of the case-aides referred Mr. Lerman to the Tuesday Club, so that he might be in the poetry group. Nearly blind, more than half-deaf, he sat next to me, breathing heavily, his hands palsied, his body leaning over to hear me better, causing a good deal of anxiety among the women, who were afraid he would fall over. His presence brought out all their motherliness; and, in fact, he could have so easily become the focal point for all our attention and anxiety, that I had to tear myself—and the group—away from him, who sat in our midst pulling us towards him, and insist that we go on with our work, and give Samuel Lerman every opportunity to participate, but that we not sit there waiting for him to collapse.

It was difficult, with him sitting next to me, so obviously ill, aged, decrepit; it was hard for me to concentrate on anything else. His physical presence weighed on me, pressed in on me, and moved me intensely. He made me uncomfortable and filled me with a desire to stop everything and nurse him. However, we carried on.

I don't know how much he heard or caught of what was going on. He held the xeroxed copies of the poems half an inch from his eyes and read them over while we spoke.

"Can I talk now?"

"Wait till Leah finishes."

Then he had the floor; he half-stood up, and made the following speech:

"Comrades, let me call you comrades, I see a group with more souls than bodies, if not for souls you wouldn't be interested in poetry.

"A poet can be the one who cannot write. A poet can be the one who feels and observes. I will disregard the proper forms of a few things I read."

He turned to me and asked: "Should I correct them?"

No, I said, they're fine as they are.

"I will disregard this. Also, disregard rimes. We want new modern forms. It's not to repeat what A, B and C said better. My suggestion as an ex-editor and as a Yiddish poet is this: anyone who feels to write should start with it, souls tell you what to put on paper. Start to be new. Start to do what you feel. Disregard what is old-fashioned, go on with it, don't look for rimes, it's not a must, your souls need to show out, do you agree?"

Leah: I threw all rimes away and it came out good.

Lerman: Yes, give us something new, something your soul tells you to put on paper, we're living in a new world. New blood, new feelings, new poems! Oh, I am proud to see a group interested together to listen and learn.

The group applauded him enthusiastically; the old man nodded and nodded, delighted.

It was so sad! So vigorous a mind in such a decrepit body—his voice was shrill and cracked, he had to screw up his face into a grimace to get out the words, he could not hear what others were saying, he could barely see—but how alive he was!

Lerman sat down and remained quiet. About half an hour later he wrestled his body out of the chair. He said: "I hope you help one another."

Dora quipped, with evident affection, "Yah, we'll go straight to heaven."

Lerman went around the room, shaking hands, and everyone stood up to shake his hand and say a good word to him. Rose asked "How old are you?" screaming it into his ear.

Lerman (and I'll never forget the silly and touching voice he answered with): Over twenty-one.

When pressed, he answered, "Four times that plus five."

Eighty-nine.

As he left, in answer to something someone said, Dora said: "*Dos is gold*" (That is gold). When Rose tried to help Lerman put on his jacket, Dora intervened: "Let be—he has one head."

One Head and Two Hats

Shortly after Lerman finished speaking, Pincus, an earthy, angry, stocky old man burst into the room, screaming at the top of his lungs: "That guy wants to walk off with my hat, he won't give me my hat, stop him!"

Pincus has started or at least added fuel to the fire of more than one fight, so initially I was merely annoyed at him for disrupting the group. I quickly saw that he was implacable, disturbed and perhaps justifiably indignant. I saw, moreover, he would in no way leave the room until he got justice. It was for him a deadly serious matter—his hat, after all. All right, I would go and see what was happening.

A slight man was standing at the door—a man I've seen in the crowd week after week, noticing only the grotesqueness of his thin wizened face, and his manner of total incomprehension of all that is going on around him. He sits with his wife—equally grotesque, a small woman with a burst of shockingly artificial red hair. He carries his head slightly thrown back and peers out at the world from half-closed eyes: what you are aware of is a pair of nostrils, turned out to the world as if in a perennial state of beclottedness, gasping for air, and half-slits of eyes that have as much trouble looking as the nose does breathing.

A crowd collected to witness the scene. Pincus too ran up, demanded the hat, and the thin man—he is brain-damaged or in some other way impaired—had the manner of a long oppressed victim who for once is going to stand up for his rights. No, it was *his* hat, and he would not give it up, people were always trying to steal his hat, and he would not, he *would not*, let it happen this time. And what about the hat on his head? Yes, that was his hat too.

Before the thing was settled there was a fist fight, an unsuccessful attempt to involve his wife, who would not leave her cardgame; futile and half-mad negotiations—finally Pincus grabbed his hat and ran.

Back in the poetry group:

Sol: The man claims both hats and he only has one head, he has one head and he's looking for another hat.

Dora: No, he's looking for the *head* he doesn't have.

In the ensuing discussion, Dora turned back criticism from the wife by saying: "She tries to keep him in shape, she watches him at every step, she's so worn out with straightening up after him."

The Snout

I had brought in a passage from Loren Eiseley's *The Immense Journey* to read to the group, and though it was late, they asked to hear it. The passage is a strange combination of Conrad's *Heart of Darkness* and Michelangelo's *Creation* and tells of the exigencies that forced the fish which Eiseley calls The Snout on to land. It is one of the grand moments of Life, a moment of Creation, when out of ooze, out of conditions certain to cause the extinction of a species, Life emerges.

The discussion of the passage was centered largely on the issue of belief, on Genesis vs. Darwin, on faith vs. open-mindedness.

Yetta, who was quite secure in her belief that "we come from God," could enjoy it "like a fairy-tale." But Dora could not, she spat out the word "Darwin," and that settled the matter.

I said I was not interested in changing anyone's beliefs, and I was quite content to view Eiseley's landscape imaginatively. I said, of course, that I happened to believe in the truth of the passage, but that I didn't think it was necessary to do so to enjoy and be moved in the passage, just as one can find *Macbeth* meaningful and true without the belief in witches. The passage was vivid in its imagery, set in an unfamiliar landscape, and provided us with a pole for identification: the fish is, after all, an immigrant who survives—a fact not lost on Libby and Florence, both of whom responded to the heroic values implicit in the passage.

Dora was still naturally vehement. "If I believe the Jew is the sacred being in God, how could I believe in Darwin?"

And yet, she was also curious: the group's interest in the passage, and their strong appeal to her to keep an open mind, was an invitation. She appealed to the man. "Sol, what do you think?"

"Well, Dora, I have an open mind."

"How many inches?" (General laughter.) Dora spread her thumb and index finger to indicate something small in size.

Sol: I was never a reader, I never had time, now I want to learn, I want to keep an open mind. I think: Leave an opening, don't have a one track mind, or just one idea.

Someone was going to interrupt Sol, Florence I think, to defend Dora; but Dora didn't want defending. "Let him speak," she said.

Sol, like most of the group members, has enormous respect for Dora's quickness of wit, for her articulate and coherent point of view; he gave her unabashed praise.

Dora is an innately modest person and felt uncomfortable with the general onslaught of praise she now received.

Florence: I admire Dora because she has the courage of her convictions.

Rose: I disagree with Florence, you can't argue with a fixed mind, a mind with one idea, convictions can close your mind, but Dora has a superior mind.

Florence: When you reach Dora's age, maybe you'll be the same.

Dora: I was a *chozzer*,* a free-thinker, now that I'm older, I'm *frum* (pious).

---

* *chozzer*: literally, a pig. In this context, it means a person who eats ham, or what the Eastern European Jews called an *apekoires*, a person who violates the laws of Kashruth; in short, a free-thinker, an apostate.

At the end, Libby spoke about the virtues of open-mindedness and the equally valuable but different virtues imparted by conviction.

As we broke up, I asked each group member to do what Leah had done: seize something spoken in today's group and use it as a starting-point of a poem. I repeated Lerman's words about soul-dictation and I also said that if some image or idea in the Snout passage took hold of them, they might write about that. I suggested to Dora that she expand her incisive and funny statement about the two-hatted man missing a head into a poem or story.

Here, then, is what came in:

Jealous Husband

I am trying to analyze the man who insisted to get another hat in his possession although he had his own hat on, that man is not stable in his mind.

He has a skeleton in his closet, now he is looking for a hat to complete his thought, to catch the man about whom he is thinking.

He summarized that his wife is involved in it, and when the fuse will give him the signal he will do something to his wife, I chill when I think about it.

His wife is a lady devoted to him, she copes with the circumstances.

—Dora Brown

Our Twilight Years

I have a great deal of respect & admiration
    for Mr. Lerman's knowledge & wisdom & yet
    his presence left me feeling very disturbed,
      reminding me these
                are
                  our twilight years.

I guess in Mr. Lerman I saw what might happen
    to us—too proud to admit we can't hear
    or see or even walk without some assistance,
      reminding me these
                are
                  our twilight years.
I keep thinking that aging & retirement is such
    a slow process, that we fail to realize it's
    happening. It seems but yesterday that

we were important in our fields—accomplish-
ing & achieving our goals—until we meet
up with a Mr. Lerman & realize that the
burdens & responsibilities are no longer ours,
reminding me these
                    are
              our twilight years.
                         —Rose Kitzinger

Learn from One Another

Four score & five
yet keen of mind
But proud & stubborn
& willing to give
his knowledge to all
who would but listen
to him of failing hearing & sight.
Should we not bear with him?
For do we not in time
go the way of all men?
Proud am I to know this man
    Should we not all?
                         —Sol Ehrlich

Genesis

It was neither the beginning nor the end of time.

The eerie winds blew violently, the sun was torrid,
the earth parched—there was not a bit of greenery.

The pools of water where the fish lived were infested
and turning into mud, the fish had to escape or die.

One creature in the form of a fish with one small
lung and snout stumbled its way to land on its fins.

It hid among the rocks to protect itself from
the glaring sun.

By the time the fish would have returned the
mudhole dried up.

This creature was able to adjust to land and after
billions of years finally became man.
                         —Florence Friedman

The First Fish of the Human Race

In our poetry workshop last Tuesday, Marc, our coordinator, spoke about a book in which the author gives an account of his scientific research and of his conclusion that man has stemmed from a fish—namely, a snout. The group listened attentively and with great interest while Marc read a paragraph slowly, giving us every opportunity to absorb each word and to ask questions as he went along.

The author described a mess of ooze which remained in a fish's habitat after it had been drained completely of the water. All of the fish, big and small, young and old, suffocated and perished in the layers of mud, except for one snout. God had willed it this way, the snout thought, and he would have to fight for survival.

With all his remaining might, he tried to extricate himself from the slush that had engulfed his brethren, but without success. With unwavering determination he continued to fight his way out of the mire. First he raised his left fin, then the right fin, he stirred gently, he squirmed, wiggled, shifted from side to side, twisted, pushed with his tail, stretched his neck, struggled, and maneuvered his next moves, until he finally rose to the top, shaking himself furiously, but completely exhausted.

Inch by inch, painstakingly, he made his way, with great difficulty, along the muddy surface, passing hundreds of bodies of his deceased relatives and friends. He did not look back. This was no easy task, but victory was his.

The snout was now alone in the world, the only survivor, and he was to be the first fish of the human race. So God had decreed—his future was predestined.

Who can say where we would be today if it were not for the unceasing efforts, courage and perseverance of the lonely snout?

—Libby Schindlinger

The Beginning & The End

It was strange, indeed, to learn that we are
the remote descendants of the Snout.

To it, we owe the birth of the brain, small
though it was.

It was strange, indeed, to learn that we might
never have existed, but for the Snout, who managed
to survive, in mud and slime, when all about him
creatures were dying in this G-d forsaken swamp.

164

We heard about the birth of man's brain,
going back three hundred million years to the Snout.
   And it was strange, and it was interesting.
We saw and felt compassion for a man who insisted
that another man's hat was his—though his own was
on his head. Nothing could convince him that both
hats were not his.
   And I couldn't help wondering why a brain
that took millions of years to formulate in a fish
could deteriorate so rapidly in a man.
   And this was sad, and this was discouraging.
                                —Rose Kitzinger

The Young Israel Group

First Session: The Steam and the Wind

This was the first meeting of a new poetry group, and the seven old people in the room had no idea of what to expect. I wanted to launch into a poem as soon as possible, to give them the feel of creating together; but I waited to feel my way to an opening that would come from them.

I was curious about the ideas of poetry they brought with them into the room. Most said it was a strange thing to them. When I asked, "What is poetry?" they spoke of "thoughts" primarily, and "ideas." I mentioned that Karl Shapiro said that "poems are what ideas *feel* like."

Ah, feelings. Yes, feelings! Poems have feelings in them. What else? Sylvia Berell said: "A poem is something with a repeat!" Repeats of all kinds: I spoke of rimes, parallelisms, key-words, sound chimes. Sylvia: "And alliteration!" Quite so. But what is alliteration? No one quite knew. I said: " 'When to the sessions of sweet silent thought, I summon up remembrance of things past . . .' Can you hear it? The repeat?" "Yes, the *s*," said Leo.

I asked: "What does the repeat of the *s* feel like?" Quietness in the room; you could hear the sound of the steam coming up, a slow steady hiss, very comforting.

"Listen," I said. "What do you hear?"

Leo heard steam.

"And what does the steam sound like?"

The steam sounds like sounds of warmth.
The steam sounds like steam coming up.
It sounds like the joy of being warm.
It sounds like someone's taking care of us and bringing us
heat in this building.
Steam is the sound of energy.
Steam is a feeling of comfort.
I would say: Steam is a good feeling if it comes at the
right time and the right temperature.
Steam is like the warmth of welcome coming out of the cold—
like a friend embracing you.
   —Leo Rogers, Ben Silverstein, Sadie Aschendorf, Florence
     Novodoff, Rose Krantz, Sylvia Berell, Yolanda Wisokolsky.

The group's first collaborative poem arose naturally in answering my question. Each one, in turn, simply stated what the steam sounded like to him. There was no need to explain the procedure for making collaborative poems. They caught on at once. As they dictated their lines to me, I occasionally read back what had been said thus far, and hearing the previous lines provided the impetus for the next speaker. Like the assignment itself, each line flowed naturally from what had come before.

During a silence in the writing of the steam poem, I heard the wind howl outside in the street. Well, it was obvious: "What does the wind sound like to you? Let's sit and listen."

Ben, after a moment, said, *"Nischt du."* Not there. I assured them, if they waited for it, the wind would come and they would catch its feeling and sounds if they kept their ears cocked for it. "Let the wind just happen." And, of course, it did—coming after the long anticipatory and contemplative silence, with a howl that evoked an excited "There it is!" from Ben. "Shhh," said Sadie, steaming at Ben for disturbing her concentration. Clearly, the interest of the group was awakened, and the poem sprang directly from their absorption.

Shhh, you can hear the wind.
The wind is blowing.
The wind is whistling through the trees.
The wind is coming to the window.
We had the wind that was shaking & shedding all the leaves.
I stood by the window, the wind was going through the

house, I have loose bricks, and the wind was shaking in the window.

The wind is blowing out the Sabbath candles.
The wind dries out the wet ground.
I often wonder if the wind doesn't have a message.
The wind has caused all the leaves to come tumbling down.
The wind causes disaster.
The wind blows dust in your eye, it happens.
The wind keeps us indoors, the wind dries out the air.
The wind uprooted the tree and disappeared.
—Leo Rogers, Ben Silverstein, Sadie Aschendorf, Sylvia Berell,
  Florence Novodoff, Rose Krantz, Yolanda Wisokolsky.

The wind released their whole imagination of destruction; and they made, in their second poem, a perfect companion piece to the sheltering indoor warmth of the steam poem.

Second Session: Leo's Story

There are some groups in which nothing gets written, and this was one of them.

We began by reading "The Steam" and discussing it. Here was a poem, ours, and we could get a sense of poetry by seeing what our poems were.

Sylvia: It's immediate.

Sadie: It's got a sing-song quality.

Leo: A poem is a picture of my feeling.

Leo said he had been thinking of steam all week, and had thought of many things. Where steam is important: trains are driven by steam, and ships. "A bakery can't exist without steam. When you see rolls shiny and round and soft, this is a credit to steam."

The group began asking Leo all sorts of questions: "How are bagels made?" "What does the steam do to the dough?" "I'm a baker, I'll be happy to tell you." He explained. And then he said: "But now, when I'm alone, look out! Everyone is for himself."

He said he was depressed now.

Sylvia: You should sing. When I get down, I start yelling my head off.

Bella: When I'm depressed, I walk out and talk to a friend. What else do I resort to? I play a record.

Leah: It's not permanent.

The group then asked to hear about what was troubling Leo, and with tact and gentleness drew forth a heart-breaking story.

Three months ago, Leo was more or less compelled to put his wife in a nursing home. She has "fluid on the brain, and it accumulated, it pressed and it pressed. The fluid has to function there like the heart has to pump. Now she doesn't talk sense. It's incurable. Four months I took her to the bathroom three times a night, cooked meals, nothing hurt." He lifted up his arms in an attitude of hopelessness—showing us: See, they are empty.

What crushed him was that the retirement he'd been so much looking forward to has been taken away from him: his wife gone mad, and his entire union pension—something he had worked 37 years for—gone to pay for her medical care.

Leo received a lot of praise, support and sound feedback from the group. Their involvement and the good things they said to him moved me as much as he did.

Third Session: Signs of Death

Leo began the group by saying that he had been troubled all week by the thought that he'd taken up too much time.

"Oh," I said, "so you're not important enough?"

Sylvia: I went back and I told Sadie: a man told us about his sorrow and I felt we all profited by it.

Ben quoted something in Hebrew, and then said it was good he had gotten it off his chest.

With this everyone agreed. Sylvia and Sally Levine both said they held things in, and admired him for being able to speak.

I said, since part of his worry was that he had taken us away from poetry, that he had brought us much closer to it, and explained what I meant by this: that the poem begins with the beginning of a person's true talking.

We then started to read and discuss "The Wind," which carries so many associations of disaster.

The ever-present subject of death came up, and Jean Blough

said, "I don't think death is terrible, it's an end of a process." I grabbed my notebook and started transcribing her words and the dialogue that followed. Leo, wounded by the on-coming of a sudden calamity, opposed Jean's attitude of acceptance with the image of the sign in the wind. "Signs of Death" records their difference in attitude toward death. It is "a conversation poem"—the spontaneous utterance of four persons speaking to be heard, and not for the purpose of making a collaborative poem. If their talk is poetry, it is because Leo and Jean were thinking in images; they both committed their feelings to a single image, which they developed logically, but in diverse directions. This is, in its basic form, the "technique" of Donne.

Signs of Death

I don't think death
is terrible
It's an end
of a process
It's a rest

Supposing a sign
is hanging loose
& the wind tears it down
It kills a person
I don't agree
it's a natural thing

It is a tragedy
I lost a brother
he was 21
& my grandfather died that week
aged 50
The rabbis came & they said:
A man lives 70 years
He lived the unfinished years
of his grandfather
And how did my father live?
He lived a nice few years
after them—sick

Even if a tragedy comes to you
it builds character
if you accept it

A sign falls
& a person hasn't had all of life
How can you prevent it?
How can you avoid it?

It's a question
of accusing the wind

The sign
didn't have enough strength
to withstand the wind

The person was innocent

Gene says it's a natural thing
Leo says it's a terrible tragedy
Look how fortunate we are
to sit here
& convey what life tells to each of us
We are fortunate at our age
to sit here & relate these stories.
—Gene Blough, Leo Rogers, Sadie Aschendorf, Mrs. Mandel

Mrs. Zimmer, a newcomer in the group, broke into the dialogue, heedless of what anyone else was saying, and with an apparent great need to talk, poured out tale after tale of loss. The story about the brother who died young, told in support of Leo's side of the argument, the darker side, was her opening wedge. She then rushed from one fragmentary event to the next, not giving anyone a chance to respond to her, and ignoring them when they did.

I found it difficult to listen to her. I stopped transcribing the conversation, and only resumed when Jean Blough had picked up its broken thread. My first response to Mrs. Zimmer was negative: she had jolted everybody out of contact. She had broken up the clear line of an unfolding thought, broken the quiet concentration that spells communicativeness among people and the environment in which the words of the poem are spoken between them. It is a fragile thing, much to be desired, this openness and responsiveness and clarity. And when Mrs. Zimmer began speaking, to me it sounded as if a belligerent and miserable roar had spoiled the loveliness of interchange in the group.

The group, however, was quicker to tune in with sympathy to this strident, outraged woman. They listened, as she rambled on, but they also, when they began to get a clear idea of the attitude out of which she was speaking, challenged her. Jean Blough was particularly firm in her gentleness: she asked Mrs. Zimmer if, among all the losses she'd suffered, she had never had gains and happy times. Yes, she conceded, her son's Bar Mitzvah.

"Hear also the other side. Concentrate also on the happiness you felt at your son's Bar Mitzvah. That is a salve for the sore."

I intervened, after my initial annoyance abated, to ask Mrs. Zimmer if she had heard what the group members had said to her. She claimed she did, but obviously disregarded them and their attempts both to console her and give her a more balanced view.

The group ended with Sadie's saying to Mrs. Zimmer: "Look, you've had a lovely span of life. Look how fortunate we are to sit here at our age and relate these stories."

Fourth Session: Hard Things

Today we met upstairs in one of the *shul** classrooms: grade-school desk-chairs, into which the old people climbed and looked like prisoners. I felt uncomfortable looking at Sadie and asked her if she wanted me to bring her a regular chair from the "Mizrachi Room," today occupied by the *shul's* accountant. No, she was quite satisfied as she was. We took the be-marshalled chairs, broke their ranks, and made a circle.

Leo introduced us to a handsome woman, a neighbor of his, Dorothy, who insisted on sitting next to him—a desire for closeness picked up by all, and one in which Sadie took apparent pleasure: signs of life.

I said a few words to Dorothy about the nature of the group, that we read poems, talked about them and about ourselves, and out of that talking we made new poems.

Then I asked them to try something with me. I asked them to think of hard things, hard objects. Sadie, when her turn came, after hearing the first round of hard-words—stone, brick, iron—said, relishing the words: "Hop-hornbeam!" That released something; the words became more interesting: "plastic cubicle, ceramic

* *shul:* synagogue.

172

mould." It was, once again, Sadie who made a leap with "hard disposition." At several points I read back the list. Sadie seemed ready to quit after "radiator." I said it was precisely at this point, where she thought she'd run out of things to say, that the interesting things would come. A new burst of energy brought: golf-cart, keyboards of pianos, hard reds, steel traps for animals. And then I read the whole catalogue back to them:

Hard Things I

Brick, wood, graphite, stone,
chair, iron, steel, gold,
metal, marble, glass, silverware,
frigidaire, plastic cubicle, safe, hop-hornbeam,
ceramic mould, radiator, shovel, hard disposition,
golf-cart, milkbottles, drums, hard reds,
diamonds, automobiles, TV, hard school tasks,
steel trap door, bank vault, hammer, planes,
hard pipes, keyboards of pianos, mountains & pencils,
oranges, steel traps for animals, mean characters.

I said a few words about form in a poem, that it is some principle of limitation that the poet decides to live with, to stick to, and asked them to speak about the things that were hard for them to live with, keeping in mind the objects in their list. "Hard Things II" is what came out.

Hard Things II

I might as well hit my head against a brick wall when I'm low.

It takes so little to be kind than mean, you go much further with the kindness.

Life makes it very hard for me to go on living.

You dig your grave with your teeth.

I finally made up my mind to climb the hard mountain so I could be nearer the stars.

I find it very hard to live: the steel trap of loneliness closed on me.

To fight to free the steel trap of loneliness, to get to the normal part that is missing—this is hard.

It's hard for me to move away from my grandchildren.

It's hard for me to take this changing world, especially family life, now there is no family life, everyone's out for himself.

I could never say that.
I'm unlucky in a lot of ways, but I'm the luckiest person in the world in my children.

For my son it's too hard to pick up the phone once in two weeks, that's hard to take, and I take it.

He comes on Sunday and he says: "Fix my pants." Last time I took it to the tailor.
Yes, let him pay.
My mother said: Have a big family so you'll have one who stays close, but they moved away.

Look, we're all blaming the young generation.
We built up a hard chain that we wanted our children to live by, it has to be broken.
We have to cut through hard chain and give our children a chance to express themselves and live their own lives.
We have things to fall back on, so we'll make them feel we haven't lived in vain.

But the children are making mistakes, foolhardy mistakes, money mistakes, and it hurts you.
My daughter-in-law bought silverplated lead doorknobs for the bedroom.

Cut your chains and let them go.

Whatever they do, they throw out things that happened to you.

You heard the expression: Button your lip? I say: Button your lip.

This belongs to the place we call hard.
When you can't express your opinion, it's very hard.
Times change as the family gets older.
You have an idea and you get an answer: "I'm old enough to judge for myself, leave me alone."
And this is one of the hardest things that belongs to the hard things.

My son is a college professor, too much education has broken
the ties.

Cut your chains and let them go.
If they make their mistakes, they have to pay, it's their
life, believe me, I made mistakes of my own.

You'd like to make it smoother for them.

No, we all have to learn the hard way.
  —Leo, Ben, Dorothy, Sadie, Sylvia, Florence, Mr. Glickenman

As in "Signs of Death," the point of concentration, the force
that drove the making-of-the-poem forward, was an important
difference in attitude.

Florence began the real dialogue of the poem by lamenting
the change in family life, and complaining of her son's distance
from her; she found and evoked a sympathetic response from
Sylvia, who blamed the loss of family closeness on "too much
education."

Sylvia, so responsive to others, needs to be encouraged to
speak of herself. After blaming her children for making "foolhardy
mistakes," she wouldn't go on, until encouraged to do so, by myself
and Sadie. "What kind of mistakes?" "Money mistakes." Could she
tell us more about it? "My daughter-in-law bought silverplated
lead doorknobs for the bedroom." Yes, now it was vivid.

It was Sadie who challenged Sylvia, telling her to "cut the
hard chains" to her children; and Dorothy challenged Florence.
The active interchange of the session took place between these
four women, two of whom accepted the separation from their
children, and two of whom felt hurt and embittered and critical
of it.

Dorothy emerged as a strong presence in the group. She presented herself in a balanced way that immediately won her re-
spectful attention: she was both unlucky and lucky; unlucky in
having had to tend to a sick husband for many years, lucky in
feeling sure of the love of her children. At the end of the session,
in response to Florence's story about a nephew who neglected his
mother—a story which reinforced her complaint against the un-
kindness of children—Dorothy opened up to the group and told us
two crucial facts about her life. She had tended a sick husband for
many years, and yet for twenty years, during the time of his illness,

she had always consulted him on every decision, so that he would feel useful and needed. And of her children she had neither asked nor expected that they take on her burden; she had refused to be supported by them, preferring to earn her own living.

At noon, when we had to stop, she came over and thanked me and told me how glad she was Leo had brought her. Sadie, standing next to her, and sharing her attitude of acceptance, also said she felt the group had been a good one.

And Leo—for the first time since I have met him—did not speak in a flat, depressed voice, a voice full of smothered tears. He smiled, seemed vigorous, relaxed. He said something, I forget the words, which let us know that his friendship with this neighbor—whom he was now looking out for—was doing him good.

Fifth Session: Images of What We Wish

We read "Signs of Death," and I ask: What about the voices? How many different voices do you hear? Lottie touched on this by saying, after first hearing the poem: "It's about one thing, but the same thing has a different meaning for different people, it affects them differently."

The discussion of "voice" flounders around for a while, until Sylvia, who is quite perceptive, grasps the flow of the poem, that it's a debate, resolved by the intervention of a third voice, which accepts the difference.

Leo, in speaking of the two contending voices, is still taking on Jean's view of death, saying of her view, "It could be changed to see the way things really are—the way really things strike and hurt."

What is interesting in the poem is the way the argument is carried in Leo's image of the sign in the wind—the image is picked up and used by the opposing voice: image, then, is not inherently rooted to a specific meaning, but creates specific import. So what's an image?

Ben, who rarely speaks, says: "We are created in God's image." Definitions follow, Leo then speaks of an image as something he forms to satisfy a wish, and the poem flows out—an I Wish Poem, of all things. Koch was, obviously, on to something: the group hit

176

upon this much-used poetry workshop formula by themselves. And why not? If I had offered it, I would have felt: old hat. Coming from them made it interesting for me again, showed me, once again, there was something very unused-up about it.

Images of What We Wish

We were created in God's image.

An image is a spirit.

It's a picture, a likeness, an image is a similarity.

There are father-images and mirror-images.

An image is a shadow.

An image is an imitation.

An image is like a wish that I would wish,
something that would be good for me and I have an image of it.
It depends on what I would like to imagine.
It depends on what I would like to have or be with.
Since we were all waiting, hoping and praying,
that there be peace with all the good things that come
with it, my wish is that there be an end to the war.

I wish for no more envy and to live without envy.
Envy's a sin, you don't know what you envy one with.

Friendships are what I wish for.

I wish for humility, and no fears between men.

To have a good old age, you have to wish for it.

I wish we would have a program so that old people
could enjoy the life they have.

For me to be happy I wish for an understanding
with the younger generation.

   —Lottie, Ben, Sylvia, Sadie, Dorothy, Leo

The rest of the group was a treat. Sylvia took out a poem she'd brought in to read, one that is famous in the senior citizen club

177

circuit. The gist is: I grew up wanting a college education, good clothes, and so forth. "All I got was words." Then follows a string of Yiddish proverbs about how to be a good person. The poem is both ironical and yet what the old people call *haymish*.*

I heard mostly the irony; so, when I asked them to explain the poem to me, I was a little surprised by what they said. For Leo, the poem spoke of "the value of good advice according to the old tradition." I heard the speaker saying he was shortchanged, also.

Lottie said: It shows we didn't need toys. We had feet and faculties and used them.

Sylvia: We are instilled with motivation and were religious. On Sabbath we sat and sang by the piano.

Sabbath recollections flowed, a fertile field, I realized, for later harvesting. The memories were fairly general, now, it being late in the session and in the afternoon after a particularly gruelling day in the club: the ticket-chaos again. Nonetheless, I heard their passion, and think good poems and lively memories might flow from it.

Leo said, "I have a memory, on a different subject, it's about two words. When I said to my mother, this was in Europe, 'Mama, I'm hungry, I want to eat,' she said, 'Eat bread.' I asked, 'With what?' 'With tongue.'"

Tales of poverty and Sabbath, brief hints, followed. Sylvia remembered a song she'd loved, one of Morris Rosenfeld's sweatshop poems, "My Son," and sang it. Leo sang an old Yiddish immigrant song about factory girls drudging away over sewing machines, near a green wild forest. Lottie, who knew Rosenfeld, recited the song he wrote addressed to his cane.

The session ended with a clear mandate to bring in Rosenfeld.

Item: In speaking of the wind, Leo said it was the destructive element. Sadie replied: "You can't have sweet grapes without the wind."

At the end of the group, we stood around talking. Leo was in the next room, putting on his coat. Dorothy said to Sadie: "Wait till I get him home." Sadie laughed. Dorothy: "Oh, don't worry, I'm too old for babies."

haymish: familiar, intimate, lovable, warm.

Downstairs, in the gym where the larger group meets, Sadie came up to me. "I wonder when we're going to go to a *chassaneh*."*
She looked overjoyed at the romance.

Before he left, Leo came up to me and said, with a certain amount of pride, "You know, yesterday I went to hear Richard Tucker—and *I enjoyed it*." He was beaming. I slapped him on the shoulder. I was also happy.

He was referring to what had been said in the second session of the group. He had said he was so depressed that even going to the opera had lost its flavor for him; he had gone the day before, and the music hadn't touched him. This had always been one of the great pleasures of his life.

At the end of that earlier session, I had said: "It sounds like you're doing a lot for yourself now, just carrying on, and taking care of yourself. That's your work for now. And I'm sure that some day—you won't even realize how and why it happened—you'll find that you're hearing the music again. It'll happen so simply you won't even think of it, and later you'll realize what happened."

So today he was telling me, in a full one-line conversation, that what I had said had happened; and, he was, in his way, thanking me.

Sixth Session: Greenhorns and Sweatshops

The Sweatshop
Corner of Pain and Anguish, there's a worn old house:
tavern on the street floor, Bible room upstairs.
Scoundrels sit below, and all day long they souse.
On the floor above them, Jews sob out their prayers.

Higher, on the third floor, there's another room:
not a single window welcomes in the sun.
Seldom does it know the blessing of a broom.
Rottenness and filth are blended into one.

Toiling without letup in that sunless den:
nimble-fingered and (or so it seems) content,

* *chassaneh:* wedding.

sit some thirty blighted women, blighted men,
with their spirits broken, and their bodies spent.

Scurf-head struts among them: always with a frown,
acting like His Royal Highness in a play;
for the shop is his, and here he wears the crown,
and they must obey him, silently obey.

— Morris Rosenfeld
translated: Aaron Kramer

We began with words: "blighted," "scurf-head"—since clearing
up the "hard words" for people whose native tongue is not English
makes the difference between comprehension and boredom.

Sylvia was quick to "see the picture" presented by Rosenfeld's
poem; and only she knew that blight was a disease of plants, and
scurf a morbid skin condition. It was Ben, however, whose English
is perhaps the most broken of all, who pointed out the appropriate-
ness of calling the boss a scurf-head: he is the head of the shop,
and his bad case of dandruff tells us what kind of head he is—a
"dirty" one.

The Rosenfeld poem immediately touched off his first memory
of America: the scene in the cap factory; and he spoke out his poem.

Greenhorn

I remember when I came here
I went to a cap manufacturer.
The shop was dark & the people wore caps
that covered their eyes
so the glare wouldn't come in
from the little lights.
Is this what I came for?

I saw people really sweating.
The men who worked by the machine
where they blocked the hats
just wore pants, no top shirts,
& they were covered with sweat.
To me—I just came over from the other side—
it was so strange.
Is this what I came for?

And then I see in the street
a man sits in a chair
& another man cleans his shoes.
Is this the golden land?
You never saw this in Europe
that a man should shine
another man's shoes, only in the Army
where the soldiers shined their officers' boots.
To me—I just came over from the other side—
it was so strange.
Is this the golden land?

I remember them getting off the boat.
They said they were looking for Gold Street.
—Ben Silverstein

Ben had never given of himself so freely; had confined himself, in the past, largely to quotations of a fitting Hebrew verse, traditional lore, and kept silence, though avidly interested in what was going on. Today he brought his wife, and it was she who provided the wonderfully sad and funny conclusion of the poem: "I remember them getting off the boat. They said they were looking for Gold Street."

Sadie, American-born, of fairly well-to-do people, said, "There are conflicting stories of Jewish life," and told us the story of her grandfather, born in Austro-Hungary on the same day as the Kaiser Franz-Josef, and therefore, despite his religion, commissioned to be mayor of his town: for everyone born on the Kaiser's birthday received a commission—Jews not excepted. Happy days! She also told us that "the opposing army" marched off with her grandmother's candelabra (bearing the royal arms) four times, and four times her grandmother went to H.Q. of the Austro-Hungarian army, after it had vanquished the enemy, and had her candelabra returned to her.

Leo asked me if we weren't getting away from the subject, which was the "worker's conditions" before the unions were organized.

I asked him if that was what he wanted to speak about.

He did, and told us a story that for him epitomized the conditions of a workingman's life"—the story of how his hand got caught in the conveyor belt.

A Workingman's Life

I was a baker, a mixer, making the dough, scaling
it, and dividing it into weights.

And I had two men working with me, a scaler, who
put it on the conveyer belt, and a rounder.

The men took the dough and put it in boxes and
stacked it up high.

I was watching the scale, there is an adjustment
to control the weight, the mixer is responsible for
this.

The conveyer belt was slippery, I wanted to stop
the belt from being so slippery, so the dough wouldn't
get stuck to a pocket.

I dusted the bottomside with dough, and my hand
got caught between the roller and the belt.

I yelled, I made a loud noise, but the two men
couldn't hear me.

The switch to stop the machine was on my right,
and my right hand was caught, I couldn't reach over
there with my left.

The two men, their minds were on their work, one
taking the dough and putting it on the scale, the
other putting the pieces in containers and stacking them.

The belt was still slippery smooth, I'm pulling
my hand out, but the sucture of the belt is pulling it
back in.

I put the whole weight of myself on the floor.
And the weight of myself got me out of the belt.

—Leo Rogers

This evoked several stories about injuries sustained while
working in sweatshops: Gussie's hand had been ripped open;
Florence had an aunt who had a needle in her hand for twenty
years.

Leo then remembered another story, and I asked him if he
would write it himself at home. "It's too much work, the way I
am now, it's not like it used to be."

Today, everything for Leo was hard. It was hard for him to
help give out theatre tickets; hard for him to understand a poem in
English; hard to write.

Marc: Well, for a lot of people it's harder now than it used
to be. Does that mean you should not go on doing anyway?

Mrs. Silverstein: My brain used to work normal, I wrote good letters to my daughter, now my handwriting is sloppy, my brain doesn't work normal, but I write.

Leo said nothing. He was clearly depressed again. After the session, I found a few minutes to speak with him privately. He had gone to see his wife yesterday and, seeing her drugged up, in urinous garments, had completely demoralized him. He had protested against the treatment she was getting in the home, and was angrily told not to interfere; and, if he couldn't "co-operate," not to come back. It sounded horrible.

Dorothy was also in the poetry group, but she said nothing; for some reason, she had not come to the club with Leo today. His buoyancy of the last session, as well as the outgoingness between him and Dorothy, were gone.

Before he left, I told him again I was interested in seeing his story; and that if he didn't feel like writing, I would like to hear it next time.

Between Fay Silverstein's comment and the end of the session, we stayed pretty much with the poem. Sylvia was particularly perceptive in picking up that it moved forward through a series of contrasts and incongruities: drunkards on the first floor, a *shul* above them. But why does Rosenfeld make the sweatshop "higher"? Ben quoted Scripture, in Hebrew, saying that "justice to widows and orphans" is what counts, and generally caught the drift of Rosenfeld's spirituality, which is that of early Hasidism and the Baal Shem. It turned out that Sylvia's son had written a book on Hasidism, which she promised to bring in; and Aaron Kramer, the translator of the poem, was a cousin of Lottie Jacobs. So there was time out for the national pastime of Jewish mothers—*kvelling*.*

Meanwhile, back at the poem: more contrasts were gathering to a head.

Ben: He says "higher" because those people are higher who are working for their bread.

Sylvia saw that the workers appeared content "with their spirits broken," because the foreman was on their backs all day.

Gussie: Inside, they're boiling, busted, and broken.

*kvelling: feeling proud.

And "Corner of Pain and Anguish?" After a lot of discussion of the meaning of the words "pain" and "anguish," Lottie *saw* it: "It's a place, like where two streets come together!"

Sadie: It makes you feel depressed—it's enough to make you go out and do something else.

Yes, that was Rosenfeld's point, but, I asked, was this a depressed man talking? What was the tone of voice of the speaker?

I read the first stanza, with its bald nouns barely receiving the benefit of a single ameliorative article, and caught the quality of nouns that explode into their sentences. "Rebellious!" said Sadie. "This is a rebel talking."

Leo: This was before unions and the fighting, before the organizing—to make things better we had to pay, we paid a lot.

Seventh Session: The Shorel Manor

Sadie began by saying she had something to "confess." "Last week when I said, 'You'll have to kiss me good-bye,' I heard giggles. That annoyed me. I didn't want to sound kittenish, I wasn't trying to be kittenish, it wasn't kittenish."

Kittenish? What was this all about? At first it wasn't clear. No one remembered anyone giggling when Sadie discussed her desire to be in the arts & crafts group, which meets at the same time as the poetry group, and said to me that I might have to kiss her good-bye.

Then I understood it all, and I simply said, "I understand what you mean," and that finished it.

It is clear to me that Sadie was feeling affectionate and playful, in relation to me. She is a handsome and attractive woman, I like her, and I think it is clear to her that I do like and appreciate her. What I realized was that she was feeling anxious lest her statement be mistaken for a come-on, for sexual feeling. Kittenish. She presents herself as a woman of dignity, intelligence and competence; she is a rather handsome elderly woman, and I imagine she must have been lovely and appealing when she was young. I wonder if, when younger, she was kittenish at all! I think not. All of this makes me appreciate more the gaiety and sparkle in her when she came up to me and said she wondered when we were going to go to a *chassaneh*. She is, obivously, aware of sex.

Mrs. Zimmer came in when we were discussing Ben's "Greenhorn." The idea being developed was that of joy in the new homeland: kissing the earth on arriving in America, or in Israel; anecdotes of immigrants dancing and yelling for joy.

Enter Mrs. Zimmer, shrill, embittered, narcissistic, willing to take offense at anything; she pays attention to no one and nothing that anyone else says, and uses a word as an excuse, a point of departure, to launch into a tirade. Everything she says sounds like a tirade. On coming in, hearing the word Israel, she began a long story about a wedding she'd gone to in Israel, talking breathlessly, angrily, in a loud voice, almost screaming, jumping from one anecdote to the next, mentioning family names and dates and shuffling and juggling scenes and characters—incomprehensible.

Quietly, I said: "Mrs. Zimmer."

"Don't you Mrs. Zimmer me."

She didn't want to be interrupted, obviously angry about the last time—the one previous time she'd been in the group, a few weeks ago—when I'd intervened and spoken to her about her non-stop manner of talking and said a few words about the purpose of the group.

"Last time it was Mrs. Zimmer this and Mrs. Zimmer that, I don't want you to Mrs. Zimmer me."

As patiently as I could, I told her she had broken into a conversation and that I felt it was important for her and also for the group that she find out how to listen to others.

She got angry and offended and sulked. My feeling of dislike for her was quite strong; I, too, was feeling angry; I have felt angry before in a group, but I have never keenly disliked one of the group members, or felt that it was futile trying to reach them. I made the attempt, and now I have been wondering all week how to handle the issue this raises for me. In the group, my strongest reaction to her was: get her out of here, she's spoiling everything. The others sat with tight lips while she was carrying on. They clearly didn't like what was happening, but weren't going to say it.

Later, however, they did.

We read William Carlos Williams' "To a Man Dying on His Feet."

—not that we are not all
                    "dying on our feet"
                              but the look you give me
and to which I bow,
                    is more immediate.
                              It is keenly alert,
suspicious of me—
                    as of all that are living—and
                              apologetic.
Your jaw
          wears the stubble
                    of a haggard beard,
a dirty beard,
          which resembles
                    the snow through which
your long legs
          are conducting you.
                    Whither? Where are you going?
This would be a fine day
          to go on a journey.
                    Say to Florida
where at this season
          all go
                    nowadays.
There grows the hibiscus,
          the star jasmine
                    and more than I can tell
but the odors
          from what I know
                    must be alluring.
Come with me there!
          you look like a good guy,
                    come this evening.
The plane leaves at 6:30
          or have you another
                    appointment?

The emotional tone of the conversation that followed was
affected by Mrs. Zimmer's volcanic presence. It was slower than
usual. Then, as interest in the poem and what it was doing began
to quicken, things became a bit livelier.

There were some problems with the poem to work through.
It was, surprisingly to me, unclear to all of them. I asked: "Who's

speaking? And who's he speaking to?" They had gotten it all confused, thought the poet was speaking of himself, or that "the world was going on a trip." The basic human situation of the poem had to be clarified. Ben and Sadie were particularly keen in getting at what was going on; and, when Sadie, naming the tone of the poem, said that the poet was trying to give "consolation" to a sad old man he'd caught sight of, and that what he felt on catching sight of him was "compassion," she had the grin of someone who has successfully riddled-out a riddle. Yes, a solution. The group had tried to get me to explain the poem. I had told them I was certain they could work it out themselves. Ben and Sadie enjoyed a kind of triumph in having done so.

I said: O.K., the sad old man is sitting on that chair, next to Ben. What do you say to him?

Ben began the Shorel Manor poem, to which his wife, Florence and Zimmer contributed.

Shorel Manor

Don't be foolish, raise yourself up
There are hopes yet
Even if you are financially short
there is a place for you
We wouldn't let you die or get so lost
Listen! We'll send you to the Shorel Manor!

You'd have people your own age to talk to
You wouldn't have to be alone there
You'll find someone suitable to yourself
They get married there

The meals there are delicious, they cater to you
Some people have to take pills
They have it down on a list and give them to you
During the day you have snacks—coffee or tea
In the night there's entertainment
If you're short Welfare will pay
It's $115 a week, two in a room
People are sociable, it's worth while living
In the afternoon in bad weather they show you movies

You can get interested in art
If you don't like art you do something else

like writing poems
If there's nothing you like to do
you can always do T.V.

There's always something going on in an old age hotel.
—Ben, Florence, Fay Silverstein, Mrs. Zimmer

After Florence contributed her line about finding someone suitable, Mrs. Zimmer gave her one in-contact line, "They get married there!" and launched into another angry story, it wasn't quite clear what it was about, but this time both Florence and Sylvia spoke up. Florence said she was getting away from the subject. Sylvia, who had been particularly peeved at the first intrusion, spoke firmly and clearly about "not going off" the way she did.

Mrs. Zimmer, on the way downstairs, seemed friendly: that is, she told me once again about her planned trip to the doctor, and at lunch she brought me pictures of her grandchildren. I was touched. Her need for recognition is enormous, insatiable. In the group, she appears to be relentless. Perhaps, though, something happened today. She took in the group's feedback—and was not put off.

Words to a Sad Old Man (I)

My suggestion to you is this:
go down to Miami and stay in one of those hotels
   for retired people
Be among your peers, keep moving
Try to be active in the hobbies you did in your youth
Get up from that chair and go out
Travel a bit—even if it's just to the Bahamas or Freeport
Take small excursions—not beyond your limit.
                —Sylvia

Words to a Sad Old Man (II)

Don't be afraid of life
You're living in America
We Americans will take care of you
Your life hasn't been in vain

You've contributed a lot to America
Just be happy in your relaxation
And make up now for the things you didn't do
when younger

—Sadie

Eighth Session: Turning On The Sadness

Ben reads a folk song that he and his wife have translated
from the Yiddish:

Child's Lament

Mother flew away
I didn't cry
She will soon come back
That's what I thought then
And she will bring me lots of toys
While she promised me a good thing
Yesterday was tomorrow
Now it's night again
Where is mother now?
I lie and wonder
Today is after tomorrow now
She is not here yet
I look at my watch and count every hour
I look in the window
And I run to the door
Mother dear how lonesome
I am without you.
Translated: Ben & Fay Silverstein

Nothing happens. This is not the first time I have been aware
of a certain stiffness, a lack of responsiveness, in this group. It has
often hung there—some obstacle, some quite definite thing, holding the members back, keeping them each sitting inside a larger
silence.

The discussion of the poem that followed was, in its own way,
interesting, but not worth reporting here. I asked questions, the
answering of which illuminated the poem for them. It was the

classroom atmosphere that Sylvia, in particular, is comfortable with. Her response to the poem was: "The child must grow up and face facts." She did not at all register the shifting tones of the poem, the child's growing realization of loss. Sylvia was already providing the antidote, in the monotone of the "realist," the stern pragmatist. Sylvia's tone, I realized, has had a decisive impact on the group. Intelligent, quick to grasp the "meanings" of things, she is also a woman who insists on staying within very definite emotional limits: this was to become the central issue of the group.

In stating what the poem was about, Sylvia finally said: "Death approaches." Well, an opening! She immediately added: "You get over it." As if she couldn't afford to linger even for a moment in the sadness of death's approach—or rather, in contemplating the child's growing awareness that death has come and gone.

Sylvia's brief relapse into affective utterance was enough to set Florence off, and she spoke vividly of her own childhood awakening to death.

Early Sorrows

My mother took us to visit my sister, and we peeked
in the hospital window.
I remember a thin white face looking out of the window.
We couldn't afford a funeral, they put her in a box
on a cart.
My brother and I were standing at the window when they passed.
I got the point: she'd never come back home, but my
brother never realized it.

One morning I saw the baby in the carriage and the next day
they said he died—he wasn't even circumcised yet.
He was lying in a corner on the floor, in-between
the man's legs.
I was a curious child, but they pulled me away, and
that was the last I saw of him, a seven month baby.
My mother said her dead children would be living if
we had the medicine we have today.
It was destiny: we all slept in the same bed and I
always got well.
Why? why? why them? Why didn't Dore live? She had
a happier disposition, she would have been happier than I.

I saw too deeply into things.

190

I remember one morning my brother didn't want to eat his egg.

My father said: Do you want a fire-engine?

He ran out and got it, and my brother ate the egg.

For an egg, he spent three dollars.

I sat there. If I said I wouldn't eat, they wouldn't have bought me anything.

I was never thin, I was packed like potatoes.

That's how I was hurt, he was the weaker, he got the ice-cream cone.

Always it was the underdog that got it, he got the milk and the cake.

He knew how to play them off.

Today he can't eat enough. I yell and scream at him: "Diabetes runs in the family!"

—Florence Novodoff

When Florence had reached a resting-place in her talk, I looked about, saw Leo had drifted off, and asked: "Leo, where are you?"

He wasn't interested.

Why not?

He was going to outdo Florence in childhood misery. "You said your father got your brother a fire-engine to make him eat an egg. I didn't have that luxury."

He then told us of the extreme poverty of his childhood and revealed, in passing, his abiding love and reverence for his mother. "My father was a mason, that's season work, in winter there was no work. My mother was a weak woman, she would grind groats on a *zdorna*—two heavy stones you grind by hand—it's made so." There followed a long loving verbal blueprint of this old Russian hand-mill, clearly an object evoking a lot of strong feeling for him. "It was hard work and the end was when bill time came her customers couldn't pay. She would leave portions of food by the door of poor people who couldn't pay. When she died, they told us what she used to do. And she used to teach poor children how to write Yiddish."

I was curious if Leo saw any connections between his mother's means of earning—or not earning—a living and the fact that he had become a baker. In response, Leo told us the story of his first difficult unsettled years in America, moving from job to job, until his brother finally taught him how to be a "mixer" and took him into his bakery.

But the main issue was: why had he not been interested in Florence?

"I'm not used to these kinds of discussions—I'm in a depressed mood."

Sylvia was quick to chime in: "Yes, we want happy things."

Leo told us that yesterday, in the blackout, he had become "so panicky," and when he went to turn on his radio and found he had a "dead radio," he had felt "so confused. I'm different now. My kids want me to visit my wife every day. And I'm so confused. Should I come here or go there? And what about the shopping? I can't adjust myself to the shopping. I wanna be here and I wanna be there."

Sylvia said, "For a woman it's easier. Men have a harder time adjusting themselves." To the loss of a spouse, she meant.

Sadie: Sylvia feels, "Let's get on with things."

Sylvia: I've been unusually happy, sadness is no good for you. On the TV if I see a murder, I turn it off, I can't seem to face it.

I told her that my feeling about her in the group was that when she saw and heard something that was possibly upsetting, she turned it off; that she was treating people in the group as she treated her TV, and that she had shared something important about herself with us. But I also expressed my concern for the effect it was having on the group.

Sylvia: Well, I just couldn't spill my heart out. When I'm blue, I sing, I throw it out that way.

Marc: Is it garbage?

Sylvia: My grandmother said, "If you cry, God gives you something to cry for." I never thought about it before, but why do you think I can't seem to face it?

Sadie: Look at men. They were brought up not to cry—listen to what Women's Liberation is saying about that.

Florence said she went to sad movies in order to cry; and Leo said he listened to sad music to let himself cry.

And that's where we got to: something had happened, and the group members were talking to one another, questioning, relating experiences, and challenging an attitude that has been growth-inhibiting for the group.

I said I felt something important had happened today, a kind of breakthrough.

In the group, Sylvia had been quite open in her impatience and in stating what she was holding back: personal statement, feeling, tears. My questioning her attitude, and the group's response, told her that her grandmother's ban against crying was an outdated edict. She left interested and, apparently, ready to question. I said, among other things, that life included sad things and it was natural and appropriate to feel sad about them; and, in fact, the only way to get past feeling unhappy over the unhappy facts was to let oneself experience the sadness: to have, in a word, a good cry —and be done with it, or more done with it than one could have been if one held everything back.

Leo, in the course of the discussion, realized that his "lack of interest" was not caused by Florence's talking about a "depressing" topic, but rather, his inner grief, his difficulty in making decisions for himself right now. I reminded him of how at one point he had not been able to take any interest in opera and then, later on, he had been once again touched by it. I said I thought it would be good for him to try to stay in touch with what the other members were saying, to become involved with their feelings and lives, but also that it was understandable, given his situation, that this would be a hard task for him now.

Ninth Session: From a High Place

Today was a short session, and it was all workshop. I began by saying: "Imagine yourself on a high place and you are looking out."

I made a few suggestive comments, without in any way filling in a landscape or providing a leading emotion. I said that literature was full of famous and quite literal "world-views," a world seen from some high place.

What were some of the high places they had looked out from?

Florence suggested an airplane and spoke of her "joyous" feeling at looking out and seeing the Alps and the clouds. This immediately touched off other associations for Leo and Ben, but I asked them to focus for the time being on high places.

Sadie spoke of Mount Mitchell and of her memory of being surrounded by clouds there. Several other suggestions were offered: ski lifts, Masada, Mount Sinai, Everest, skyscrapers.

Taking the pulse of the room, it was obvious that Sadie's "mountain" suggestion evoked strong images from most of those present, with Florence's airplane as the runner-up.

I gave them the first line of a poem: "I stand on top of Mount Mitchell and I look out." Then I asked each one to close his eyes, imagine himself on top of the mountain, contemplate the vision, and say what he sees and hears. The poem came quickly, rarely lapsing into the anecdotal elaborations. There was a high degree of interest in the subject and in making the poem. Several times somebody slipped into the past, and I immediately repeated the verb in the present tense, to remind them that it was happening here and now, that we are now on the mountain top, looking out, seeing and hearing. When I re-read the finished poem, Sylvia was highly pleased; said she thought it was the best thing the group had done; that "it really flows."

The "Airplane Poem" followed the same pattern, except Leo did not participate. When the group was finished, he said he had had his own and different airplane experience. I asked what it was, telling him to put it in the present, as an event happening to him here and now. Using his hands dramatically, to indicate the shaking of the plane and the heaving of his innards as the plane dropped, he presented his poem—acting it out.

Airplane Poem I

I'm flying high in the heavens and I look out.
I see the fleecy clouds below me like snow banks.
At the top of the clouds I feel like I'm standing still,
    I feel like the plane may drop, it's just not flying.
It looks like the surface of the moon to me, I want to get out
    and walk on it.
The first cloud I see is like a huge bird flying alongside
    the plane, and the second cloud is a ship, I am sailing
    along beside it.
I look at the clouds and I can't believe my eyes—there's a city
    in the sky.
Clouds form into a vision and I see a distant city.

194

I see the clouds opening and twirling and I wonder: what's
    behind it?
There is an opening in the sky and I look down and I see the
    Grand Canyon like a tiny snake.
I know there are cars and people down below but all I see
    are little ants going all over.
All of a sudden the sun comes through and I see the earth
    surrounded by a rainbow.
Coming back to New York I see the whole city spread out
    before me, I see all the lights of Manhattan, I see
    all the bridges, everything is so clear, it's a homecoming
    and I am thankful.
                    —Sadie, Sylvia, Florence, Ben, Rose

Airplane Poem II

I'm in a single motor plane in a deep seat with my head
    sticking out.
I feel like I'm in a canoe and I'm floating in it with nothing
    solid underneath.
I am looking out and everything is alive and moving in miniature.
The motor's so noisy it's impossible to hear what my nephew
    is telling me.
Before I got into this plane, I thought: Whatever will be,
    will be.
But coming down is worse than going up, I feel like I'm
    falling, dropping in an old style elevator, fast,
    with my insides coming up into my mouth.
                            —Leo Rogers

Mountain Top Poem

I stand on top of Mount Mitchell and I look out.

And I can see nothing, I'm covered with water, my head
    is in the clouds.

After 3 minutes the clouds disperse, and looking down
    I realize the height I'm at.

And the first sound I hear is the sound of the chickadee,

they are coming up out of the laurel bushes,
the mountain top is covered with laurel bushes.

I feel glorified standing on top of the mountain, and fearful
about going down.

I comfort myself, saying: I got up, I'll probably get down.

I feel as if I'm all alone in the world standing on top of
the mountain and wondering at all the marvels.

Suddenly I hear the rush of waters—the waterfalls
and the rapids below.

I wonder how Moses got to the top of Mt. Sinai and how
he was able to survive 40 days without food
and water—it's still a miracle.

I feel the wind blowing down and the quietude and the
presence of God surrounding me.

I see the water, I'm standing on a ledge and the water
coming down from the upper heights is like a
bridal train.

I feel if I stretched out my hands I would reach the heavens.

I feel I'm closer to God.

      —Leo, Rose, Fay, Sadie, Sylvia, Florence, Ben

Part Three

The Poems

The Good Girls

We were watched like hawks.

I came home from a wedding it was a 2 a.m., my *Zeida** carried
on it was something terrible, "A girl has to be in the house by
ten o'clock," I did what I felt to do.

When I came home from a date, my father used to yell:
Bummerkeh!†

It made me think: My father doesn't want me to have a good time,
he spoils my time.

So I slept over a girlfriend's house where they didn't care when
we came in.

I wasn't allowed to go to a Chinese restaurant—*and I didn't.*
Years later, Mamma says: "You should have gone, you didn't
have to tell me.

I look at my sister. Now she tell us that!

I went everywhere—to cabarets—Chinese restaurants—everywhere.

I had a friend, she made a date for me and it turned out to be
the Governor's son of Puerto Rico.

So I sat in the back seat with the Governor's son of Puerto
Rico and he started to get funny. I thought: this isn't for me.

On the way back I sat in the front with the chauffeur, my
friend sat in the back, she continued the friendship and got
presents.

I didn't realize what type girl she was, I was a virgin.

If you don't have a good time when you're young, you can't
when you're old. I got heartburn again.

     —Bella Jacobskind, Hilda Glick, Vera Rosenfeld

* *Zeida:* Grandfather
† *Bummerkeh:* female bum, irresponsible girl

Self-Portraits

When I graduated high school in 1919, the training school took one and a half years. Papa was begging me to go and become a school teacher, but I was afraid to be an old maid.

If I had gone, it would have changed my whole life. If I had become a school teacher, I would never have married a man like my husband.

I married my cousin—my mother's sister's son.

A fortune-teller told me that I had a short lifeline.

I got pregnant and the doctor said you have to have a *kaiserschnitt*,* I was afraid I was going to die.

I wanted a carriage with a big pink bow.

I wanted to see my daughter become a teacher.

I wanted to see her dressed as a bride, but the war came— her young man was called up and they got married in Florida.

I lived through all the bitterness from the Polacks.

The college boys tore out half my uncle's beard—that's how they used to celebrate their independnce.

And if the Jewish boys got better marks, they used to beat them up—three rows of ghetto-benches in the back.

I was a Zionist all my life—that was like my cradle.

The first kibbutz in Israel was Grodovna, we started the work there. The land was bepestered with malaria. From all over they came, the first pioneers, the college boys, from Russia. Herzl said on the map we should only be a dot but we should have our own corner.

Look at how much honor Israel gives us. That's how we live.

—Vera Rosenfeld, Hilda Glick, Bella Jacobskind

* *kaiserschnitt:* Caesarian section

I Remember

I remember when I was a little girl when my mother held me in her arms and held me close to her breast, I was the baby of the family, perhaps that's why I'm somewhat spoiled.

I remember with what joy I planted a couple of trees in Israel on the border of Jordan and Jerusalem.

It was in the stones, you put the tree in the stones and it grew.

During the war for independence, this forest was a camouflage from the Arabs, they shouldn't see what they were doing.

I remember my father speaking: he was nine months old when the Bolsheviks took his father to prison. His grandmother went to the store for milk and when she came back he was gone.

I remember doing volunteer work in Bellevue Hospital and I took an abandoned gypsy girl to the playground.

When she returned, the other kids asked her: "What did you see and what did you get?"

"I saw the sky."

—Hilda Glick, Bella Jacobskind, Stan Malkin, Vera Rosenfeld

Standing Up for Myself

If you stand up for yourself at this stage of the game, they ask: "Who is she? What does she want?"

What may seem important to you may not interest the other person—she may be thinking of her new dress or her card game.

Life taught me to stand up and take care of myself, my mother died when I was two years old.

A policeman knocked an old Jew down in the street and the *Yiddlech** ran like field mice. I went over to help him up, and the policeman threw me in jail.

My mother taught us to accept everything.

What were you taught—to stand up for yourself?

The children of today are wonderful, today these children think for themselves and do what they want.

But the older people don't agree with them.

We have to let them do what they want!

To be *mishugana*† hippies?

Long hair, and if they want to go barefoot, let them—you can't condemn them.

We didn't prepare such a wonderful world for them—look at the wars we made.

There always was war and there always will be war.

Absolem was his father's enemy & went out against him & David cried when he lost him.

Cain & Abel—they had a whole world to share & they slayed each other.

Here's what I say: Kids of today, you're smart, you're making the most of every moment, you do what you want—you have to break with your mothers.

                    —Vera Rosenfeld, Hilda Glick, Bella Jacobskind

* *Yiddlech:* little Jews
† *mishugana:* crazy

Hours

Hours alone with nothing to do, nowhere to go, no one to speak to.

Hours when my husband looks at me and says, "I married the right
    woman, to me she is my companion, my love, my life."

The hour of my first day in Jerusalem, over there is the Yad Va Shem,
    all the remainings of the ovens, it's on the highest mountain in
    Jerusalem, it's King David's tomb.
And an Arab soldier was walking back & forth.
And the first thing that struck me: a bar of soap, wrapped in the
    traditional colors—and printed on it was: *Reine Judenfetz.* *
The most terrible thing I saw was the sacks of ashes—and the little
    children's shoes all bloody.
The horror is finished, I want to say what I lived through
    that moment.
I lost my group and met an Old Jew who told me: *"Genug,
    takhter kind, kum aroise."*†
Then our guide was running up the mountain and when he
    found me, he said: *"Boruch Hashem,*‡ I found you alive. If the
    Arab saw you alone, you would be shot."

I broke out with a cry, it was a cry from bitterness & pain, the pain
    of 2000 years and of all the people lived through—fire & torture.
It took a long time till that cry stopped in me.

* *Reine Judenfetz:* Pure Jewfat.
† "Enough, my child, come out."
‡ *Boruch Hashem:* "Blessed Name," thank God.

Hours when I was dressed as a bride, when I walked down the aisle
    I didn't realize that the rest of my life would be spent with
    this man.
The rabbi was playing with his gold watch & chain and I didn't
    realize I was giving my whole life to this man, I knew nothing.

Hours of pleasure when I discuss with my daughter the books that
    we read together and when she agrees with me—but mostly
    there's a gap.

Hours of frustration when we are both in the kitchen and he's
    in my way and I'm in his way.

Hours of discovery when I act without thinking.

Hours of anger when I'm held back from doing what I want and
    my whole chest is a fist.

Hours of self-doubt, hours when I feel small & unimportant, when
    someone other than me gets excited about something mundane
    like going to work or drinking orange juice or wearing a tie that
    matches your suit or hearing Chicita Banana on the radio, she
    knows what she's here to say, it always surprises me that she
    recognizes her role on the earth, I could never say that.

Hours of happiness when I sit at the piano and I play the old
    lullabies.

                    —Bella Jacobskind, Hilda Glick, Allen Greenberg

An Old Habit

    When I got married, I was living in a furnished room.
I had to cook in Mama's house and bring it back to my husband.
    The woman I lived with said: "I don't mind if you
cook in my kitchen. But a man is like a monkey. If you don't
train them in the beginning, they'll never be trained. Why
don't you go out and eat in a restaurant once a week?"
    If you don't go when you're young, you can't go
when you're old.
    That's the way we make our life.
    A man gets accustomed to economizing and that's the way
he goes through life—and a woman too.
    And I say: Enough is enough! How much longer?

                                        —Vera Rosenfeld

Forgetting

There will come a day
when you won't remember what happened yesterday
You go to the drawer
& you don't remember what you came for
Deterioration of brain waves
I speak to oldsters & they all complain
about losing their memories

> Don't have that on your mind
> Don't fear it.

My friend's name
vanishes from me

> It won't get worse

We want our faculties
Face the truth: it has to.

I got an uncle 85
He's got a better memory than I
He's got thick hair
He talks on any subject
But my friend's name vanishes from me

> You won't get worse

I want my faculties
Face the truth: I have to.

Eleanor Rooseveldt said she took garlic pills
When a reporter asked her what for
she answered: My memory!
I didn't waste any time, I ran
I always fall for these things

In all these years—in 45 years
of working in a factory
I never forgot my apron
But when I started taking the garlic pills
then I forgot it.

My daughter—I hate to tell her the bad.
But to you: I can tell this.
> —Beatrice Zucker, Hilda Glick, Marc Kaminsky

Regret

I should have done something
with my life
to make money

All my friends are buying homes in Florida
I wish I had enough for that little one-room in Florida

If I sing a song
I swear by my child
a woman who directed plays 20 years ago
tells me: You have a better voice
than many of those on Broadway

I could have done something with myself
I made beautiful beautiful things
Poems from the time I was fifteen
In feathers I produced original designs
I thought I'd outgrow it
when I came to the age of the end of reproduction

At 45 I could still make designs in feathers & poems
Now I've lost my desire to do it

I'd love to spend my last years in Florida

I remain an *alteh shnorrekeh**

I should have done something with my life to make money
                                                    —Beatrice Zucker

* *alteh shnorrekeh:* old beggar-woman, old chiseler

206

Florida

Florida!
I wish I had enough
for that little one-room
in Florida!

To me Florida is the last stop
    and I want to keep moving.
—Beatrice Zucker & Vera Rosenfeld

My Religion

We are all connected to God with invisible wires
When we lie or deceive
we twist the wires
& make it impossible for us
to reach the Supreme Mind

I'll even tell you my true age
That's how much I believe in the truth
I'm 78
                                —Beatrice Zucker

Dancing

Would you believe that I danced this morning?
We had the TV on this morning
& I heard the music & it went to my feet.

I went this way & that way
I lifted my hem up & I kicked like this
I did kicks like a chorus girl.

In Florida that's what I do
& they shout: Take it off!
I unzip my dress—just a little.

Would you believe that I danced this morning?
My husband with his stroke he *kvelt** & told me:
Hilda, you'll never get old.

                                   —Hilda Glick

* *kvelt:* glowed with pride

The Welfare Band

I was in The Welfare Band
I couldn't play the first note
because it was pitiful
to see the old folks dance

Their attempts
their slipping around
their movements
their figures were so grotesque
I couldn't take it

—Sylvia Berell

Time Out of Control

Time is fleeting ever so swiftly
Don't like me
Don't love me
Just understand me.

Runaway horses!
Runaway team!
Runaway days
Runaway years
Runaway laughter
Runaway tears
Runaway hopes
Runaway fears:
A sudden halt before the
edge to death
To let life give its final
breath!
—Leah Cahn

Vienna, 1938

I lose at same time all my furniture,
my husband & son.
I am always in black, always in black.
Not for him, for my son.
I like him better than my whole life.

Why I am so *umglicklekh,** so unfortunate?
On the street everyone sees how poor I am.
Why I suffer like this? There is no God.

Then I dreamed I saw God.
I had a dream & I saw God
like in a movie where the boy goes to heaven.

I am so comforted.
I come to America.
I work in a factory.
I work & I work.

I wanted very much to be rich.

—Pearl Eisenstein

* *umglicklekh:* unlucky, unfortunate

Warsaw, 1943

My father died in the sewer.
He hid himself so they wouldn't carry him off.
"I want to die like a proud Jew,
not like a cockroach."

He was one of the best watchmakers in Warsaw.
He helped the boys make bombs & grenades.
They were in the sewer fighting,
& that's where he died.

—Bella Jacobskind

Palermo, 1898

I was born in Palermo, Italy.
On All Souls' Day
we would have to find a platter
with cookies & sugar dolls.
We called them *il morte*—the dead.

In my child's mind
I would picture the souls
come from the clear clouds
I watch from the distance.

—Antoinette Jackson

In Roumania

I spent my early childhood in Roumania where I was born.

On occasion the King and Queen would honor us by passing
by in the royal coach.

How grand, clean and well-fed they looked!

My brothers, my friends & I would run after the carriage
& loudly & fervently sing, "Long live the King! Long
live his dynasty!"

We were barefoot, raggedy and underfed.

Had I spent my teens & twenties in Roumania, would I still
have admired the royal family?

—Florence Friedman

Hot Sun

When I walked in the hot sun this morning I was reminded of my youth.

When life became too difficult for me to handle I would go down to the beach.

There I would lie down on the warm soft sand and gaze upon the mighty ocean whose roar filled my ears.

I would think and wonder whether the salt water, fish or tiny pebbles had been shifted by the currents from the Gulf Stream or perhaps the China seas, which I never expected to see, but I always wondered at the beauty and magnanimity of the world and its oceans.

After some meditation I would stand up refreshed and relaxed and more able to face my problems.

—Florence Friedman

Sioux City, Iowa

No matter where I go or what I do, my mind goes
back to Sioux City, Iowa.

My friend gave me a flower from her yard.
Immediately I traveled back to Sioux City, Iowa,
but to one certain spot. The field—it will
always be to me the dandelion field.

There were row upon row of wild grasses rippled
by the summer breeze. Wild flowers grew in abundance.
The smell of wild clover was all about me. Tall
sunflowers looked at me with dark beautiful eyes.

My friends and I sat hidden by the tall grass.
We made jewelry for ourselves out of the dandelion
stems. We braided bracelets and necklaces for
ourselves.

No matter what happens in my life, I go back
to the dandelion field. It is a place of hiding
from the harshness of the city in which I live.

                                        —Leah Cahn

On Monhegan Island

When I was on Monhegan Island, off the coast
of Maine, I ran across a field of yellow daisies
bringing to mind the summer I spent with my grandparents many a year ago.

I could still hear the mooing of the cows
which mingled with the mewing of the sea gulls.

—Ann Branfield

A House in Memphis

In Memphis, Tennessee
there was an ad in the paper
for over a year:
a house for sale.
And people would go down & inquire.
But every week-end it was there
for sale.
After a year
someone decided to investigate,
so he went down & asked:
"What's the problem?
Why can't you sell the house?"

The house wasn't for sale.
They were just an old lonely couple
& they were looking for company.
And every week-end
they used to have coffee & cake
ready for their guests.

—Lillian Smith

In Israel

In Israel on the border of Syria
they dried out the swamp
& they made a paradise.
It was so beautiful
I didn't know where I am.

From the swamps
with rifles on their backs
they drained it.
All the diseases
come from there.
The Arabs didn't want this
& they fought them.
Three years it took them
to dry out the swamp.

Beautiful vegetables are growing.
One place they made an artificial lake.
Big white lilies are growing over there
like Japanese.

—Bella Jacobskind

Son-in-law

I set up a good Jewish home for my daughter,
& Murry comes & everything is turned upside down,
the *milkhiks* with the *fleishiks.**
I could tear out my hair.

Better to have a friend than an enemy.
I eat with them & it's not kosher.
It's all mixed up—so what?
I go with them.
You have to go with the tide of life.
*
The boys sit ten in a group
& they make fun of their mothers-in-law.

So Murry sits & is quiet.
"You know what I tell them?
I got the biggest admiration for her
We understand each other
better than me & my own mother."
     —Bella Jacobskind

Horsing Around

My son-in-law—
all the dirty jokes he knows
he comes & tells me
& I enjoy them.

I'm not a sedate person.
    —Lilly Palace

* *milkhiks:* milk dishes and utensils; *fleishiks:* meat dishes & utensils.

218

Crazy Wisdom

I find good things
in situations where others complain
No one thing is ugly
Even a dirty thing
has beauty in it.

If I see a colony of ants
people would say Ucch, those worms!
But I stand there & I watch them & watch them
You'd be surprised
what they do—so much work, so lovely!
Is there something wrong with me?

I don't think it's real
I don't see the dirt
There's something bigger than that
I see the bigger thing.

—Lilly Palace

Old Age Home

Today I went to an old age home to do what
I could to help. This evening I am depressed at
what I have seen.

Why should we be so helpless when we live to
an old age? The vegetable too becomes spoilt once
useless with time. Except for having a brain are
we relative to the vegetable?

I looked at these helpless souls sick of body
and many sick of mind. There were fixed blank
stares in many eyes. They were waiting to be called
to their maker. Others with calm acceptance of
their fate—all wearing the same human condition.
All I could think of was *No*, negative—no is a
denial of love, of trust, of faith. No means
you are not wanted or needed, you've outlived
your usefulness.

In the past some cultures put out their old
to be devoured by wild animals or die of starvation.
We are more civilized. We let them die of
loneliness.

I want to believe that life has meaning, so
I must look for the beauty. The trees, the flowers,
the blue sky are beautiful. Come winter they too
must wither and die. For the winter of life is
cold and lonely.

Life is triumphant—death the defeated,
yet life and death are but a whisper away.

—Florence Friedman

Emotion

1.

Emotion is blurred vision. It is a hand,
a foot, uprooted grass.

It is a picture, a stray dog, an old shoe,
old letters.

Of water, it is the high, the low; of life,
the in-between. Of earth, it is upheaval.

It is the angry, the frustrated.

It is the calm, it is music.

2.

I like to shake a hand or a foot when I hear
good music.

I like the picture of old shoes or boots with
laces by Van Gogh.

I like to take a stray dog home, but there are
too many allergies around.

In life there are always the in-betweens—a
sister or a brother that is in the middle.

If you have ever been in a flood you become
very frightened when you see the water rise high.

Then you offer a prayer of thanks when you
see it become low.

The waters have vented their anger—like a
frustrated spoiled child—then becomes calm,
like soft music or the earth sinking back to its
natural element after the upheaval of a storm.

—Leah Cahn

Compassion

1.

It's flying off into the blue horizon or a cruise
on the calm seas or reclining on a soft pink sofa with
my beautiful Persian cat.

It's a doctor or a rabbi with a strong pair of
shoulders.

It's Jonathon Livingston, Seagull in flight in the
prime of his life.

2.

The water was calm.
On the deck
sitting
on a pink sofa
sat the doctor
listening
to the rabbi.

Reclining
at their feet &
looking skyward
was a Persian cat
tenderly
watching the seagulls.
—Sol Ehrlich & Rose Kitzinger

Think of Others

If we could but open
our closed unseeing eyes
to the care-worn faces that we pass
we'll recognize
heartbreak & loneliness
trouble & despair
that a word of understanding
would make easier to bear
—Sol Ehrlich

Withholding Judgment
to my daughter

1.

In the middle of the night
I sat myself upright in bed
addled by the question whirring about my head:
"Is your God faith?"

What is there to say when I myself
question myself this way?
This accusation, this great big lie
I must deny,
I must introduce myself to me.
"Is your God fair?"

I do not change my God from day to day.
I did not have a different God yesterday,
the day before, nor do I have one now.
How do I know the turn of the path, the way to go?
Time and tale have told me so.

If you would to another your belief confide
when too many of the good things in life
have been you so denied
then who is to say if you should turn your back
to go forth and seek your comfort another way?

Where did we come from,
why are we here?
Is there a different atmosphere from which we came?
Were we plummeted from the heavens,
erupted from the earth,
spewed out of the sea?
What is this life, our glorious destiny?

No more queries. I must tell myself,
if I am to have faith upon this earth
that which was instilled in me from birth.
I must believe that which is above and beyond reasoning,
believe that or my judgment reverse
that in Heaven it may be better,
yet here in Hell it is worse.

223

2.

There are two people encompassed in one body
be it spirit or conscience or whatever name you give it
they are always at odds with one another
or perhaps we can call them faith and doubt
that which accepts and that which questions
they will always be at odds with one another.

—Leah Cahn

The Tuesday Poetry Group

Marc our hairy catalyst
with kindness & understanding sits
Rose with hair & heart of gold
Bella sticking to her mold
Sol takes pride in our advance
Stable Libby's common sense
Rebecca listens hard & quiet
Ann voices her opinion long
Lillian feels beauty is so strong
Talented Leah's looking fine
Dora lays it on the line
Let me say this whole caboodle
I wouldn't change for a great boodle
If you don't like my opinion
let's get together & make a *minyon.**

—Florence Friedman

---

* *minyon:* in order to pray, at least ten men must be present; that group
of ten or more is called a *minyon.*

The Snake

Eve, you are a beautiful woman
but if you eat this apple
you will have a complexion
as rosy as the peel of the apple
& you will be more desirable
in the eyes of your husband

Your eyes will be opened
& you will see further into the future
beyond this garden

You will also learn acceptance
to accept the things you cannot change
& you will first realize that you are a woman

Just take one bite
& see the whole world unfold before you
You will realize that beyond the garden
there is a world of knowledge & beauty

You will be happy & satisfied
You will be thankful for eating it

You will become an understanding woman & mother
You will have many beautiful daughters & handsome sons
And you will be the prime woman of the world

Mother of all human life
Wife of first man
Creator of beauty & comfort
Creator of great sons & joys
eat this fruit & the world will be yours!

—Young Israel Group*

---

* Leo Rogers, Ben Silverstein, Sylvia Berell, Florence Norodoff, Rose
Katzman, Dorothy Weiner, Sadie Aschendorf.

A Prophecy

1.

Cain, you are a stalwart young man
You tend the sheep with your brother
You plow the field with your brother
Everything you do & have
you share with your brother

But you will get involved with a rage
& you won't control your temper
One day you will quarrel with your brother
over the sharing of the crops
You will realize there hasn't been an equal distribution
Your nature will be to dominate & possess
In anger you will raise your hand
not realizing what you are about to do
You will strike him & you will slay your brother

And all killers from this time on
will bear the mark of Cain

2.

You will realize you have done a great wrong
You will hurt your parents & your family.
You will be a marked creature
You will be a big blot on the world to come
You will always be in a state of repentence
Your conscience will follow you wherever you go
& you will suffer agonies of remorse
You will be degraded & dishonored the rest of your life
You will wander over the face of the earth
& all men will cast you out

You will touch individuals here & there
& they will repeat your crime

—Young Israel Group

226

I Remember

I remember when I was little I showed my mother the book of
Jean Valjean and she said, "I read it," and I was surprised
that she knew about it—and she knew Balzac too.

I remember how happy my grandson was when he was going to
have a party at the House of the Disabled.

I remember the thrill I got after going to a basketball game with
my husband and then going to Houdini's home and seeing all the
trap doors—it's been with me over fifty years.

I remember receiving a beautiful bouquet of red roses from my lover.

I remember when the Cossacks came with their horses and jumped
down from their horses and danced the *kazatzka*—it was gorgeous
music—and I heard that music today.

I remember how things have changed since I was a girl.

I remember when I went to the candystore with my nephew and the
line was busy. He was only a little boy and he told me,
"Tell them to take the clothes off the line."

My proudest moment was walking down the aisle with my two sons—
it was on the same night and they married twin sisters.

I remember what our neighborhood used to be and what it is now.

I remember when my son came out of the service, it was on
Mother's Day, he brought me roses, I'm still thrilled.

I remember when my oldest son was young and he wrote beautiful
poems, I still keep them and read them.

I remember a time when we didn't have to lock our doors.

—Bensonhurst Group*

* Bertha Treibwasser, Mary Michaelwitz, Carrie Fleishman, Lillian Smith,
Eva Glick, Anna Shaw, Lucy Celentano, Pauline Affronte, Anne Laub,
Anne Cole, Ann Magid, Ann Jackson.

If Poem

If I were the corns on Sylvia's feet, I would bark &
    I would say: "I want to walk around barefoot all
    day," and my toes would be smiling & free.

If I were the arrogant Zsa Zsa Gabor, I would kick myself,
    I would stand myself in a corner, I would hang my head
    in shame.

If I were that apple tree swaying in the breeze,
    I would drop my apples on whomever I please.

If I were the sun, I would shine brightly on the little
    kids playing at the beach, I would shine on the ones
    I love, I would shine on all of you.

            If I were a raincloud
            not a tear would I shed,
            I'd wait till all the people
            were tucked in bed.
And at night I would water the apples & orchards!

If I were a pussycat & spoiled, I would sit around & purr
    & purr—that's my spoiled cat Cookie.

            If I were a babbling brook
            I would gurgle so sweet
            & call to the weary
            to come soak their feet.

If I were the moon sailing in the sky, I would shine on
    the lovers who are sitting with their arms entwined.

If I were my unborn grandchild, I'd cry, "Lemme outa here!
    Time's up! Mama, stop fooling around!"

If I were my grandson, I would say, "Little boys are not
    for yelling."

If I were the postman, I'd deliver only the letters with
    good messages.

If I won a million dollars, I'd go to live in the place of
    my dreams.

            If I were a blank wall
            what a heaven I'd be
            for kids who do nothing
            but graffiti on me!
                                —Bensonhurst Group

Gossip

Gossip could make a lot of trouble for people
Gossip is very cruel
Gossip is malicious
Something is always added or subtracted
Gossip spills out
Sometimes its interesting
We all enjoy it

—Bensonhurst Group

It Was Fated

You see this bracelet? Thanksgiving my son came with the car,
I put it in my pocketbook.
I'll get to my son's house, I'll put on the bracelet.
The bracelet fell down when I took out the keys,
I don't see nothing.
I didn't see so I didn't see.
I was at my son's till 8:30. I came home.
I'll take everything out of the bag, I'll find the
bracelet.
It wasn't there. I called my daughter-in-law.
"Look in the couch," she said.
"O.K. Hold on. It's not there."
I walk on the steps, up and down. Maybe I lost it.
Listen! I go into the house, I go again on the
steps—*nisht du.**
Then I remind myself I heard a click. Let's see.
A little click. I go outside and right in my door—
seven hours later—my bracelet is laying.
I give a look and there it is—it cost enough *gelt.*†
And nobody took it.
I got it back, I called my daughter-in-law.
"Are you lucky," she says. "A light burning and so
many hours laying there."
It's a miracle without a dream.

—Minnie Blumberg

* *nisht du:* not there.
† *gelt:* money.

229

Recovery

A friend of mine, getting out of a cab she sees she
doesn't have her ring, it's a dinner ring, a cluster of
diamonds.

She's at a loss. She calls one sister and then
another sister, nobody saw a sign. She went here and
there, nothing.

It had a lot of snow.

She thinks maybe she lost it when she got out of
the cab.

She spent an hour looking. Right near the curb—
as bright as all the snow—there it was!

Overnight, and then with all the people going
to work, no one took it. It was meant for her.

—Carrie Fleishman

Dreams, Prayers & Visions

1. Ben's Prayer

I went to shul fresh.
They pull me out of shul.
I was more dead than alive.
My granddaughter she's a speech therapist.
You see me, I'm big like a fly.
She teaches like this—with a fist.
She takes one look at me and says: "Ain't you a fool!
Goddamn good for nothing!"
I only had 106 degrees and I start to live.
I don't wanna work so hard and I start to laugh.
They took me to the slaughterhouse.
Ten operations I had.
I said to her, "Why insult me?"
But I kiss her hands.

Listen to this!
I fell asleep, I got up—it was Friday, 10:30.
The operation was supposed to take a half hour.
It took five.

I started hollering:
God, hey you, whattaya want from me?
I don't bother you.
You are my good God.
I earned my money with my own fingers.
I never took graft.
I ate good, no garbage.
Red meat, I paid fifty cents a pound.
Anybody comes to my house goes away full.
I say it with two pair of pants—winter and summer.

2. Ben's Dream

I had a good dream. My dream was my Hershele, my life,
only one of my boys. I have twenty-one with the greats: two sons,
one daughter, so many grandsons, so many greatgrandchildren.

I was dreaming Mama and Papa came from *Gan-Aiden.**

And what do I see in *Gan-Aiden?* A line of white coffins—
shh!—beautiful Paradise!

And that guy from *Gan-Aiden* says, "You don't belong here."

"You mean in *Gehenim?*"†

I gave him a *setz.*‡

I hollered, "I wanna go home. Let me go home."

That Friday after the last stroke they pulled me—feet
numb—in the recovery room.

"Ladies"—the *shenste*§ in the world—"this is good, but
I would like to go home. Haven't I got a better house at home?"

They put a hot blanket on me and I came to life.

* *Gan-Aiden:* Paradise.
† *Gehenim:* Hell.
‡ *setz:* a blow, punch.
§ *shenste:* prettiest, loveliest.

3. Bertha's Dream

I never knew my greatgrandmother, I was named after her:
Breina.

My greatgrandmother came and brings me a baby.

"I can't take it because we don't have enough for ourselves
and the other boy."

"Look how pretty it is! Take it! Take it!"

"Is it a boy or a girl?"

"Take it. It will bring you luck."

She threw it at me and went off.

Next day I found I'm pregnant.

4. Carrie's Dream

After the war, my mother didn't know whether her mother
was living or not. I was eight months pregnant.

I dreamed I'm in shul near the altar. There are two men
handing a pillow one to the other.

The next day I told my mother the dream, and she said
one is the *kvater*°° and the other is the *sandik*.#

"Now I'm sure my mother is dead and you're gonna have a
boy and you're gonna name him Ascher Leib after your
grandmother."

°° *kvater:* godfather.

\# *sandik:* the man who holds the pillow on which the infant lies, at a
briss, while he is circumcised; the family bestows honor on the man
they ask to be the *sandik.*

5. Mary's Story

I read about a sick girl and her father was crying and crying.
He sat down on a bench in a park and he was crying.

His parents said to him, "Why do you go on crying? If
she'll be well, she'll be well, even if you don't cry. You
want to know what to do? Go to shul and pray."

He prayed so long!

His father said to him, "Get a small place and make it
into a shul and have people come and pray with you."

And that's how it was!

This is all written down on an old paper—with the picture
of the father and the daughter. It's so yellow now it's like burned.

6. Lillian says:

They call those miracles—the miracle of opening a sanctuary.

7. Lillian's Dream

Erev Rosh Hashanah they operated on my father.

I dreamed I was up in heaven and the women cried: "Hurry!
Hurry! We're getting company!"

That night my father passed away, just as everyone was going
to shul.

8. Millie's Fear

I'm reluctant
to talk about dreams
I walk to the window
& shake myself.
to forget

9. Lillian's Vision

When my grandmother passed away, I didn't go to the funeral from the home, but from our house.

It was January, a beautiful day. Some of the carriages got lost and came late.

I wandered around—what do you do in a cemetery?—and read tombstones.

I went to the houses of the dead, reading names, I went from one to the other.

A hand came out from one of those drawers and motioned me to go away.

I thought: This is ridiculous. I wasn't afraid.

I thought it was the shadow of someone standing near by.

I went to look and there was no one.

And again and slowly the hand motioned me to walk away, so I went.

This happened in the Bayside Cemetery.

10. Bertha's Dream
I hadn't seen my father in thirty years.

One morning I dreamed I made a bed with fresh linen,
with everything clean and white, and I said:

"O.K. Papa, you can go to sleep now."

That day I got the telegram my father had died.

11. Bertha's Aunt's Dream
My mother was going to have a baby.

We lived in the woods, a goy lived near us, and it was
a half hour's walk away to the others. This was in the old
country, in the town of Strelisk, in Galitzia.

My father asked the goy maybe you got a *haibam**, but the
midwife was drunk.

My mother's sister lived on the edge of town and she
sees my grandmother going by and she says, "Stop in my house."

"I have a *geviner'n*—a woman in labor, have to run."

The next morning my brother came into town and told her:
"Mama had a girl."

It was me.

> —Ben Shore, Bertha Treibwasser, Lillian Smith, Carrie
> Fleishman, Mary Michaelwitz, Millie Buxbaum

---

* *haibam:* midwife
† *geviner'n:* woman in labor